THE REDEEMED CHRISTIAN CHURCH OF GOD
NORTH AMERICA

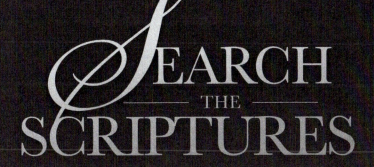

TEACHER'S MANUAL

2015 - 2016

Search the Scriptures
2016-2017
Copyright © 2016 The Redeemed Christian Church of God North America

ISBN 978-1-60924-124-7

All rights reserved. With the exception of brief excerpts for review purposes, no portion of this book may be reproduced or transmitted in any form or by any means, electronic or mechanical including photocopying, recording or by any information storage retrieval system without the written permission of the Redeemed Christian Church of God North America. Unless otherwise indicated, Scriptures are taken from the King James Version of the Bible.

Printed in the United States of America.

Published by:
Triumph Publishing
P. O. Box. 690158
Bronx, New York, 10469
www.triumphpublishing.net
718-652-7157

To order copies, please contact:
Sunday School Department
RCCG Victory Temple
P. O. Box 480098
Charlotte, NC 28269
704-552-8895
Email: rccgsundayschool@gmail.com

TABLE OF CONTENTS

1. A Life – Style of Thanksgiving — 7
2. Praise Ye The Lord — 11
3. A Heart of Gratitude — 14
4. You Must Be Up To Date – Part 1 — 18
5. You Must Be Up To Date – Part 2 — 23
6. The Integrity of God — 27
7. God's Expectations — 31
8. God Is Committed To Man — 35
9. Vessels Unto Honor — 39
10. God's Nature And Expectation — 43
11. King Asa Was Righteous — 46
12. Destiny – Definition of Discovery — 50
13. The First Quarter Interactive Session — 54

14. Enemies of Destiny — 55
15. Recover Your Destiny — 58
16. Earthly Citizenship — 62
17. Christianity And Governance — 66
18. Voting — 70
19. Divine Calling — 74
20. Everyone Has A Substitute — 78
21. Tough Job — 82
22. Danger of Drifting — 86
23. Depression In The Life of A Believer – Part 1 — 90
24. Overcoming Depression In The Life of A Believer – Part 2 — 94
25. The Fear of The Lord — 99
26. The Second Quarter Interactive Session — 103

Table Of Contents

27. Faith Not Covetousness	104
28. The Man Jesus	107
29. Like Father Like Son	111
30. Unity In The Church	115
31. Disunity In The Church	118
32. The Making of A Champion	121
33. Divine Champion	125
34. He Was Betrayed	128
35. When God Asks Questions	132
36. Angels	136
37. Lucifer	140
38. That I May Know Him	145
39. The Third Quarter Interactive Session	149
40. Fellowship With Others	150
41. Rape	154
42. Abortion	158
43. Preparing For Marriage	162
44. To Have And To Hold For Ever	165
45. Love Covers All	169
46. Parenting In The 21St Century	172
47. The Master Sculptor	176
48. Fruitlessness	180
49. The Bleessedness of Fruitfulness	183
50. Overflowing Blessings	187
51. Hospitality	191
52. The Fourth Quarter Interactive Session	195

PREFACE

The Bible admonishes us to be diligent to present ourselves approved to God as a workman who does not need to be ashamed, handling accurately the word of truth. We are to seek the word of truth, know it and in essence, we are to study the Bible to discover the treasures in it. This knowledge starts with knowing some foundational truths.

What you know determines your position in life. What you know can change your fortune. It is what you know that can deliver you from spiritual death.

Our counsel to you now and always is to continuously study to show yourselves approved to God and as you lay new foundations and repair old ones, continue trimming your lamps, getting ready for the Master. Giving thanks and expecting multiplication to begin. Thanksgiving turns healing to wholeness, invites divine visitation and precedes a new era. Your new era is here, in Jesus' name.

Pastor E. A. Adeboye

A LETTER FROM PASTOR JAMES FADEL

The Lord has been gracious to us in the Redeemed Christian Church of God, North America and we have experienced tremendous growth in our Search the Scriptures Classes.

Undoubtedly, our Search the Scriptures classes on Sundays have been an interesting and exciting forum through which sound biblical doctrines are taught and this has helped in building and transforming lives. The topics are tailored on practical Christianity and they touch on areas of our lives where we need to hear and know the truth as the Word of God prescribes.

I encourage everyone never to miss any Search the Scriptures class this year as all the topics have been carefully compiled based on sound doctrines that will help our spiritual growth and maturity to become the real man that God wants us to be.

For every diligent seeker of truth and faithful disciple of Jesus Christ, I commend this Search the Scriptures manual to you as a useful tool for your journey in the Kingdom. I pray that the Word will shine in us all in Jesus' name.

This is your year of rest, abundant testimonies, plentiful harvest and surely His goodness and mercy shall follow you throughout this year and beyond, in the Name of Jesus Christ, Amen.

God Bless!

Pastor James Fadel
Special Assistant to the General Overseer & Chainman RCCG, North America.

LESSON 1
A LIFE – STYLE OF THANKSGIVING

PRAYER POINT – Pray that the Lord will grant you the grace to make thanksgiving a permanent feature in your life.

PREVIOUS KNOWLEDGE – Teacher to discuss the last assignment with the students to list what they think can be likened to leprosy in lives from which the Lord cleansed but people are not showing enough appreciation.

TODAY'S LESSONS

1. OPENING

i. ***LESSON TEXT*** – Psalm 95:1-11

ii. ***MEMORY VERSE*** - "In everything give thanks; for this is the will of God in Christ Jesus for you" 1 Thessalonians 5:18

iii. ***LESSON INTRODUCTION*** - Abraham Lincoln in Thanksgiving proclamation of 1863 said, "We have been the recipients of the choicest bounties of heaven; we have been preserved these many years in peace and prosperity; we have grown in numbers, wealth and power as no other nation has ever grown. But we have forgotten God. We have forgotten the gracious hand, which preserved us in peace and multiplied and enriched and strengthened us, and we have vainly imagined, in the deceitfulness of our hearts, that all these blessings were produced by some superior wisdom and virtue of our own. Intoxicated with unbroken success, we have become too self-sufficient to feel the necessity of redeeming and preserving grace, too proud to pray to the God that made us."

As we study this psalm, we will see that it addresses a basic flaw of mankind – developing an attitude of 'I did it, I deserve it' rather than 'I'm thankful for it'.

TEACHER'S DIARY

i. ***LESSON AIM*** – To study thanksgiving as an attitude and not just for a season

ii. ***TEACHING OBJECTIVES AND LESSON PLAN*** – At the end of this lesson, students should be able to enumerate why God is the source of all things. They should be able to mention at least three consequences of failure to acknowledge this fact. They should be able to mention at least three reasons why God is the source of everyone individually. They should be able to enumerate at least five reasons why everyone should choose thanksgiving as a habit. The goal however is that everyone should take a decision to make thanksgiving their choice. To achieve these goals, the teacher should involve everyone in the class to participate actively.

iii. ***TEXT REVIEW*** – Psalm 95 1-11
- There is a call for us to leave our present situation of thanking God for specifics to a life of giving Him thanks at all times – vs. 1
- The call is to a joyful shout to the Rock of our salvation – vs. 1
- Coming to His presence should be with thanksgiving, which is with joyful shouts and in psalms – vs. 2
- A major reason is that God is great and a greater King than the gods – vs. 3
- God has the deep places of the earth and heights of the hills – vs. 4
- God made Seas and dry land – vs. 5
- Some ways to worship include, bow down and kneel down before God – vs. 6
- God is our God and our shepherd because we are His sheep – vs. 7
- The call to continually give thanks calls for obedience and not a hardened heart – vs. 8
- Refusal to obey is likened to rebellion – 9
- Refusal to obey God despite the fact that they saw His work is part of rebellion – vs. 9

- ○ The rebels went astray not giving thanks to God for His mercies – vs. 10

iv. **_TEACHING METHOD_** – Teacher should use discussion method for this lesson.

v. **_TIME MANAGEMENT_** – Teacher should devote about 80% of the time to lessons A and C while 20% of the time should be for lesson B.

1. LESSON OUTLINE

i. **_LESSON OUTLINE A_** – GOD IS THE SOURCE
   - ○ God is the source of all things and He created it all – Psalm 24:1-2
   - ○ Achievements by personal efforts are based on gifts and power provided by God – Deuteronomy 8:18; I Chronicles 29:11-12; James 1:17; If we fail to acknowledge this the following results may happen:
     - ◊ Conflict with God - We will think life is about what we acquire or receive while God says that life is about what we give away, Luke 12:15; Pr. 11:24; Acts 20:35.
     - ◊ In fear for life - If God is my provider then I can be rest assured that I shall not lack. On the other hand, if I am my provider, my provision depends on my not failing. Only God NEVER fails. Ps. 27:1; 46:1; 73:26
     - ◊ Ungrateful - If I am the provider, then why should I thank anybody? "A self-made man worships his creator." Luke 12:16-20

ii. **_LESSON OUTLINE B_** – GOD IS MY SOURCE
   - ○ God is greater than all human devices – Genesis 28:15; Psalm 121:4; 91:12; Exodus 19:4
   - ○ His care for me is unique – Luke 12:7; I Peter 5:7; Matthew 6:32; Psalm 115:12
   - ○ He has a special name known to Him – Isaiah 62:2; Revelation 2:17

iii. LESSON OUTLINE C – THANKSGIVING IS MY CHOICE

Thanksgiving has to be your choice because thankful people:

- Choose to focus on the positives not the negatives of life
- Find a way to turn negatives into positives. They realize that God really does cause all things to work together for good. The furnace may be uncomfortable but the product is beautiful. (Romans 8:28; Job 23:10)
- Look for the best in the world around them – often you find exactly what you are looking for. (Ps. 8:3-4; Ps. 19:1-3)
- Are grateful for what they have, not focused on what they want (see Romans 1:18-23)
- Know that life is all about God. If anyone helps us it is because God decides he should and if otherwise it is God's decision. Saul and his servant decided to go to prophet Samuel in search of his father's lost asses whereas God had earlier told Samuel the previous day that He (the Almighty) will send Saul to Samuel, I Samuel 9:5-16. God has His purpose allowing situations or challenges in our lives, John 9:1-7. Jesus knew when Lazarus died, John 11:11-14 but He did not rush to go and raise him from the dead.
- Know that our situations will not change God. He remains God in spite of our situations. He can change all situations but nothing changes Him. The response of Jesus Christ to John the Baptist's message while in prison was that Jesus performed some miracles. What a great lesson that we should thank Him in all situations
- See obstacles as stepping stones to greater heights – Genesis 37:18-28; 45:5

3. SUMMARY

We don't have any excuse not to make thanksgiving our way of life.

4. CONCLUSION

Thanksgiving should be our way of life.

5. ASSIGNMENT

Spend the next one week in the presence of the Lord giving Him thanks.

LESSON 2
PRAISE YE THE LORD

PRAYER POINT – Students should pray that God would grant them a heart to praise Him always.

PREVIOUS KNOWLEDGE: Students should explain their experience with the steps of faith they took after the previous week's lesson.

TODAY'S LESSON

1. OPENING

i. **LESSON TEXT** – Psalm 150:1-6

ii. **MEMORY VERSE** – "Praise ye the LORD. Praise God in his sanctuary: praise him in the firmament of his power." Psalm 150:1

iii. **LESSON INTRODUCTION** – God must be praised for so many reasons. Believers must find all privileges and benefits of God to them to warrant consistent praise. When one takes stock to count God's daily blessings upon his / her life, there be no choice but to praise and worship God. This would be our major focus in today's lesson. It is our prayer that God will teach us in the name of Jesus Christ, Amen.

TEACHER'S DIARY

i. **LESSON AIM** – To study on the reasons for and the ways by which believers should praise the Lord

ii. **TEACHING OBJECTIVES AND LESSON PLAN** – At the end of the lesson, students should be able to mention at least five reasons why we should praise God. They should be able to enumerate at least four methods to praise God. The goal is to encourage everybody to take positive decisions towards praising God at all times and select the appropriate method to use. The teacher should guide the class as the students make contributions.

iii. ***TEXT REVIEW*** – Psalm 150:1-6
- The chapter starts with a call to praise God. David called for praise, we know it is the outcome of his past experiences.
- The sanctuary is one of an important place to praise Him.
- Praise The Lord in the firmament of his power, vs. 1
- God deserves praise for His mighty acts. You should mention some of them, vs. 2
- He should be praised because He is excellently great, vs. 2
- Trumpet, harp and other musical instruments must be used to praise Him, vs. 3-4
- His praise should go with dancing, vs. 4.
- The praise should be harmonious producing sonorous lyric that can be danced to, vs. 4
- The praise is expected to be very loud, loud cymbal and high sounding cymbal, vs. 5
- Everything that has breath is called upon to praise the Lord, vs. 6

iv. ***TEACHING METHOD*** – Teacher should use discussion method.

v. ***TIME MANAGEMENT*** – Allocate time equally to the two lesson outlines. Teacher should avoid contributions that would lead to controversy or that would waste time.

2. LESSON OUTLINES

i. ***LESSON OUTLINE A*** – WHY WE SHOULD PRAISE THE LORD
- Teacher asks students to form a long list of why they should praise the Lord.
- Some of the expected comments should include our salvation, security, peace, sound health, victories, provisions, privilege, our family, our job, our forgiveness, mercy, love, kindness, favour and

so on for who He is - He is the provider, life-giver, for His work, greatness, power, throne and so on.
- ○ Students should read the following scriptures while teacher explains their relationship with praises. Psalm 100:3, Lamentation 3:22-23, Isaiah 53:5, and Psalm 150:1-6.

ii. *LESSON OUTLINE B* – HOW WE CAN PRAISE GOD
- ○ Students should be encouraged to enumerate some of the ways through which we can praise the Lord. The list should include the following:
  - ◊ with our souls
  - ◊ from our heart, in understanding
  - ◊ with our offerings and gifts, our substances
  - ◊ in hymns and spiritual songs with musical instruments
  - ◊ with dancing in worship with clapping
  - ◊ with rejoicing in truth and holiness. e.t.c.
- ○ The following scriptures should be distributed to students to read and comment.

Ps. 100:1-3; Ps. 9:1; Ps. 138:1; Ps. 63:3-5; Eph. 5:19; Col. 3:16, Ps. 150:3-5.

3. SUMMARY
Now that we have discussed why we should praise the Lord and how to praise Him we should begin to praise Him with all our strength in true worship and holiness.

4. CONCLUSION
Praise Him for everything.

5. ASSIGNMENT
Praise God throughout this week without asking for anything from Him. Share your experiences with the class during the next week's Sunday School.

LESSON 3
A HEART OF GRATITUDE

PRAYER POINT – Pray that the God will give you a heart of gratitude all days of your life

PREVIOUS KNOWLEDGE – Teacher reminds students of different ways people express gratitude in different cultures and what it means not to express gratitude for a gift.

TODAY'S LESSON

1. OPENING

i. ***LESSON TEXT*** – Luke 17:11-19

ii. ***MEMORY VERSE*** – "Because that, when they knew God, they glorified him not as God, neither were thankful; but became vain in their imaginations, and their foolish heart was darkened." Romans 1:21

iii. ***LESSON INTRODUCTION*** – "Thanksgiving is the art of giving thanks, or a show of gratitude and appreciation for something done to you. Why are people not showing appreciation to God? Is it that God has not done anything? Jesus Christ appreciates thanksgiving. He was surprised that only one of the ten lepers came back to express appreciation. All of them were in need, all cried for mercy, all persevered, all believed and obeyed but only one returned to express appreciation after the healing.

TEACHER'S DIARY

i. ***LESSON AIM*** – To learn about the heart of gratitude.

ii. ***TEACHING OBJECTIVE AND LESSON PLAN*** – At the end of this study the students should be able to give at least four reasons why people do not praise God and four areas that Christian seek for time to praise God

   iii. **_TEXT REVIEW_** – Luke 17:11-19
- Jesus Christ is always on the move to show Himself mighty on behalf of people – vs. 11
- All the ten men had leprosy on them – vs. 12
- They were all condemned to not moving close to people – vs. 12
- All of them cried to Jesus for mercy in their distress – vs. 13
- All of them knew Jesus Christ as a master in time of trouble – vs. 13
- Jesus saw and spoke to all of them without an exception – vs. 14
- The instruction was given to everybody – vs. 14
- All of them obeyed the instruction and all were cleansed on the way – vs. 14
- Only one realized the importance of coming back to give thanks – vs. 15
- The one who came back did it openly with a loud voice – vs. 15
- He gave the thanks with all humility; fell down on his face at the feet of Jesus Christ – vs. 16
- The one who appreciated was not very important in rank, position or anything – vs. 16
- Jesus noticed the level of the man's gratitude – vs. 17
- He got more blessings from Jesus, he was made whole unlike the others – vs. 19

   iv. **_TEACHING METHOD_** – Use discussion teaching method.

   v. **_TIME WATCH_** – Use two lessons outline standard time.

1. LESSON OUTLINE

   i. **_LESSON OUTLINE A_** – ONLY ONE CAME BACK

The reasons many people are not appreciating God could include the following:

- Discouragement and Tribulations Dan. 2:25. Daniel was a captive at the time he began thanking God. Paul and Silas in prison Acts 16:16-26.
- Lack of knowledge of God's word: Even if God did nothing for you, it is wrong to thank only those who are good to you as a child of God Luke 6:32-36; Matthew 5:44
- Taking God for granted: Using thanksgiving as a substitute for obedience. Luke. 18:9-14
- A life outside Jesus: Rom. 7:25
- Fellowship with the wrong crowd. Eph. 5:1-5
- Refusal to take account of what God has done.

ii. ***LESSON OUTLINE B*** – THE CHRISTIAN APPROACH

Some Christians limit themselves to the following situations to thank God:

- Thanksgiving as a show of appreciation for what the Lord has done, Ex. 15:1-21; Lk 17:11-19, Lk. 1:36; Lk. 13:11-13
- Some Christians rejoice when they are anointed especially in the area of deliverance. Consider Jesus Christ's view as against that of the seventy Lk. 10:17-21
- Thanksgiving is at times used as a prayer of faith, Phil. 4:6-7; Jn. 11:41
- Thanksgiving as a weapon of warfare 2 Chr. 20:20-27
- Thanksgiving as an evangelistic tool: Ps. 57:4-11; 1 Sam. 22:1-2
- Thanksgiving sustains selflessness and Humility, Dan. 2:23-24; Lk. 18:9-14; 1 Tim. 1:12-13.
- Appreciation when people are born again, Eph. 1:15-16.
- Gratitude when there is food, John 6:11; 1 Thess. 2:13

3. **SUMMARY**

God expects us to show appreciation and gratitude for His blessings upon our lives

4. **CONCLUSION**
   God appreciates our appreciation.

5. **ASSIGNMENT**
   Make a list of what you think can be likened to leprosy in lives of people from which they have been cleansed but not showing enough appreciation unto God

LESSON 4
YOU MUST BE UP TO DATE – Part 1

PRAYER POINT – Pray that the Lord will touch you through this lesson and helps you make all required adjustments that is required of you.

PREVIOUS KNOWLEDGE – Teacher should help the class to discuss what constitutes an update and in what equipment they can easily be noticed.

TODAY'S LESSON

1. OPENING

i. ***LESSON TEXT*** – 1 Kings 19:19-21

ii. ***MEMORY VERSE*** – "But as many as received him, to them gave he power to become the sons of God, even to them that believe on his name", John 1:12.

iii. ***LESSON INTRODUCTION*** – The only permanent thing in life is change. There are changes in life especially in technology, mobile phone, fashion trend and even people. Upgrades are required to keep up with better performance. In the same token, God Almighty is never quite done with us, as He is constantly upgrading us from grace to grace, strength to strength, anointing to anointing and glory to glory, 2 Cor. 3:18. Being upgraded can be very inconvenient, however the benefits far outweigh the costs. To illustrate this, we'll use the common example of a Windows PC update and draw out some lessons.

TEACHER'S DIARY

i. ***LESSON AIM*** – To study on the importance of constantly updating self, including in the Word.

YOU MUST BE UP TO DATE – PART 1

ii. **TEACHING OBJECTIVES AND LESSON PLAN** – At the end of the lesson, students should be able to explain the need for updates in a computer. They should be able to mention the fact that you must connect to the internet before you will talk of an update. They should be able to the processes that Elisha went through to connect to Elijah and subsequently obtain the double portion of the anointing in the life of Elijah. They should be able to mention the fact that updates are optional. They should be able to enumerate at least three people who willing join themselves to others in the Bible and at least two who had options to join others but failed to take the opportunities. To achieve these objectives, the teacher should engage the class using practical knowledge of downloading updates from internet. He should remind the class that only those who are connected to the internet can download updates.

iii. **TEXT REVIEW** – 1 Kings 19:19-21
   - The meeting of Elijah and Elisha was ordered by God, vs. 19
   - Elisha was a successful mechanized farmer before he met Elijah, vs. 19
   - Elijah cast his mantle upon Elisha, vs. 19
   - Elisha did not waste time in his decision to follow Elijah, vs. 20
   - Elisha requested to kiss his father and mother good bye before following Elijah, vs. 20
   - Elijah allowed him, vs. 20
   - Elisha slew a yoke of oxen, note the importance of blood, vs. 21
   - Everybody ate of the slain oxen, everyone was part of the decision as witnesses, vs. 21
   - Elisha arose and went with Elijah, 21
   - He ministered unto him, the call is for service, vs. 21.

iv. **TEACHING METHOD** – Teacher should use participatory method.

v. **TIME MANAGEMENT** – Teacher should share the teaching time equally with the two lesson outlines.

2. LESSON OUTLINES

i. **LESSON OULINE A - GET CONNECTED, STAY CONNECTED**
   - You can only receive or install updates if your PC is connected.
   - If you don't use your PC, it makes no difference if you have Windows 8 or Windows 95.
   - The moment an update becomes available; Microsoft pushes the update to all ACTIVE computers and as many as are connected to the internet will be able to download the update.
   - Likewise, you have to be saved and connected to God before there can be any updates because you cannot do anything without Him, Jn. 15:1-6.
   - The prerequisite for anyone to see the Kingdom of God is to have a relationship of second birth, Jn. 3:3-7; Jn. 5:17; 1 Pet. 1:3.
   - Elisha left his business and followed Elijah, 1 Kings 19:19-20. We must stay connected by being obedient to God because we cannot abide in sin and ask grace to abound, Rom. 6:1-2.
   - Elisha took time off to settle some important issues in his life. One of such issue is to bid his parents bye, 1 Kings 19:20-21 he then followed Elijah all the way.
   - The result was a double portion of the anointing upon the life of Elijah, 2 Kings 2:9-11.
   - Peter reminded Jesus Christ that they had left all to follow Him, Mk. 10:28-30.
   - You must seek first the kingdom and his righteousness before there can be additions, Matt. 6:33.
   - You need God to work in you both to will and to do of His good pleasure, Phil. 2:13, so stay connected. You therefore need to get connected and stay connected to God through Jesus Christ.

ii. *LESSON OUTLINE B* – UPDATES ARE OPTIONAL
   - Windows updates are optional; you can always decline.
   - The developers understand that not everyone wants an update so updates are optional to keep the customer happy.

- Likewise, God Almighty will not force Himself on us. He stands at the door of your heart knocking and will come in to those who open their hearts to Him, Rev. 3:20.
- Joshua gave a charge to the children of Israel to make a choice on serving the Lord. He made a choice to serve the Lord with his house, Josh. 24:14-15.
- Jesus Christ was clear when He said that no one can serve two masters, Lk. 16:13.
- He asked from the twelve if they wanted to continue to stay with Him, Jn. 6:67.
- Our decisions of yesterday form part of life today. Ruth decided to follow Naomi, her mother in-law, while Orphah decided to go back, Ruth 1:11-18.
- If you don't desire an increase, He'll simply keep His increase available upon request. We can all remain at the same level of worship, knowledge of the Word, number of dreams/visions per year, frequency of prayer, level of problems, etc.
- Your Up-to-Date status is completely up to you. As long as King Uzziah, though a teenager, sought the Lord, God made him to prosper, 2 Chr. 26:1-5.

CLASS ACTIVITY – The class to discuss how to be permanently connected to the internet.

3. SUMMARY

You must be connected to the Lord to be able to enjoy His benefits. The food of children is not meant for dogs, Matt. 15:26

4. CONCLUSION

Life is a product of choices, we can choose to serve Lord or not, Josh. 24:14-15. It is. We will surely make mark in our relationship with God if we are consistent irrespective of the time. God promised to vomit the lukewarm from His mouth, Rev. 3:15-16. It is good to be connected to God and stay connected.

5. ASSIGNMENT
Students should study reasons why people find it difficult to be connected and why some connections are not permanent.

LESSON 5
YOU MUST BE UP TO DATE – Part 2

PRAYER POINTS – Pray that people will be encouraged to connect permanently to the Lord through the study of this lesson.

PREVIOUS KNOWLEDGE – Class to review previous week's lesson with students. Assignment should equally be reviews.

TODAY'S LESSON

1. OPENING

  i. **LESSON TEXT** – Luke 9:59-62

  ii. **MEMORY VERSE** – "He that observeth the wind shall not sow; and he that regardeth the clouds shall not reap" Ecclesiastes 11:4

  iii. **LESSON INTRODUCTION** – Last week, we looked at the fact that we should get connected and stay connected using the analogy of a Windows PC update to convey our explanations. We realized that life is full of choices and the decisions of yesterday are part of our lives today. The decisions of today may be part of our lives tomorrow. Windows PCs use a "Remind Me Later" button. After using it so many times, the PC's performance begins to suffer. Several decisions with time as essence, Eccl. 3:1, have suffered due to many of us using the "Remind Me Later" button. Believers have done great things in the past but need updates to do greater things. This is a character flaw that affects millions of people in every walk of life. The Remind Me Later" update could include courage, patience, boldness, anointing, financial decisions and many areas of life. It is our prayer that the Lord will teach us on how to get these updates in the name of Jesus Christ, Amen.

TEACHER'S DIARY

i. ***LESSON AIM*** – To study why we should seize opportunities on updates because this will allow us do more than we have been doing.

ii. ***TEACHING OBJECTIVES AND LESSON PLAN*** – At the end of this lesson, students should be able to enumerate at least three Biblical examples of people who seize opportunities to become blessings. They should be able to explain how opportunities become effective in our lives. They should be to use at least four examples of Biblical situations where people seize opportunities to become blessings. They should be able to mention at least four situations when people were updated and were able to do more than they were before their updates. They should be able to explain how discouraged people can overcome with an update. They should be able mention at least somebody in the Bible who had an opportunity to download an update but failed.

iii. ***TEXT REVIEW*** – Luke 9:59-62
- One of those called by Jesus Christ gave an excuse of father's burial for his refusal to follow Jesus Christ, vs. 59.
- Jesus said that burial should not be an excuse not to preach the Kingdom of God to others, vs. 60.
- Another excuse is relationship with family members, vs. 61
- The response of Jesus Christ is that there is no excuse for any man to look back after having laid his hands on the plough, vs. 62.
- Such a man is not fit for the kingdom, vs. 62.

iv. ***TEACHING METHOD*** – Teacher should use participatory method.

v. ***TIME MANAGEMENT*** – Available time should be shared equally.

2. LESSON OUTLINES

i. ***LESSON OUTLINE A*** – SEIZE THE OPPORTUNITY
- PCs perform better than they were if we seize the opportunities to download available updates.

- Time and time again, the Holy Bible shows us that one way by which our Christian virtues are demonstrated to glorify Himself is to allow opportunities for us to be used.
- A small boy became a blessing by giving his lunch which was used to feed five thousand people to the glory of the Lord, Jn. 6:5-14.
- The widow of Zarephath gave her last meal to Elijah to remain alive throughout the period of famine, 1 Kings 17:9-14.
- God is giving us the opportunity to touch His heart by bringing those in need of food, cloth and home into our ways, Matt. 25:31-46.
- King Agrippa had an opportunity of becoming a Christian, Acts 26:28 but did not take it.
- Same is the case with many people today who do not give the word of God a place in their lives.
- When we pray to God for a blessing or ability, God almost immediately answers with an opportunity to manifest.
- Solomon prayed for wisdom, 2 Chr. 1:8-12, and also received an opportunity to display wisdom, 1 Kings 4:29-34; 10:1-7.
- Hannah prayed with a vow, 1 Sam. 1:10-11, and received an opportunity to fulfill her vow, 1 Sam. 1:24-28.
- Likewise, when we pray for courage, patience, boldness, anointing, fruitfulness, ability to forgive, etc., God gives us an opportunity to manifest.

ii. ***LESSON OUTLINE B*** – UPDATES ALLOW YOU TO DO MORE
   - Windows updates are critical additions to software that prevent and / or fix problems, enhance the security of the enterprise system and optimize the performance of computer hardware.
   - An update from God allows you to do more than you thought. Moses was updated with God's presence before meeting Pharaoh, Ex. 3. Daniel was updated with an excellent spirit before God was glorified through him, Dan. 5:12-14; 6:3.
   - Elijah was updated with divine power to outrun the chariots of Ahab, 1 Kings 18:45-46. The disciples were updated with the Holy Ghost before their evangelical ministry, Acts 1:7-8; 2:1-4.

- Peter's message yielded a harvest of three thousand souls, Acts 2:41.
- Five thousand were later added to them, Acts 4:4. There were constant addition to the Church, Acts 2:47.
- You are one update away from doing greater works than He did, John 14:12. Are you up to date?
- He requires you to call to Him and He will answer you, Jer. 33:3. Remember that God is the one who works in you both to will and to do for His good pleasure, Phil. 2:13.
- If you feel discouraged or defeated, you are only an upgrade away from the best moments of your life.

CLASS ACTIVITY – Class should discuss reasons why King Agrippa, Acts 26:28 would fail to take opportunities of the updates available to him.

3. **SUMMARY**

   Updates energizes you to achieve more than the current performance, you should seize all opportunities that come with updates

4. **CONCLUSION**

   Opportunities for updates are available regularly and it depends on individuals to download them. God will not force anyone to take the opportunities, the choice depends on individuals. You should look out for updates and pray that the Lord will help you to recognize them and give you the ability to take good decisions.

5. **ASSIGNMENT**

   Students should compile, individually, available updates that can help performance of children of God. They should equally give reasons why people don't take advantage of the updates.

LESSON 6
THE INTEGRITY OF GOD

PRAYER POINT – Let the class pray that the Lord will help them to believe His word and promises for their lives.

PREVIOUS KNOWLEDGE – Teacher should lead the students to review the previous week's lesson through guided questions.

TODAY'S LESSON

1. OPENING

i. ***LESSON TEXT*** – Genesis 18:9-14

ii. ***MEMORY VERSE*** – "God is not a man, that he should lie; neither the son of man, that he should repent:hath he said, and shall he not do it? Or hath he spoken, and shall he not make it good?" Numbers 23:19

iii. ***LESSON INTRODUCTION*** – Integrity is the quality of being honest and upright in character; adherence to moral and ethical principles. It simply means saying what you will do and doing what you say (Num. 23:19). There are fundamental questions to be asked about the integrity of God. Who is God? How reliable are His words or promises? Does He have the capacity to do what He has said? Are there testimonies to this fact?

TEACHER'S DIARY

i. ***LESSON AIM*** – To study about the incomparable integrity of God.

ii. ***TEACHING OBJECTIVES AND LESSON PLAN*** – Through the lesson, students should be able to understand the unchangeable nature of God and His word. They should be able to mention at least four testimonies of God's integrity. To achieve these objectives, teacher should allow the students to pray the opening prayer together. He should also allow the students to review the previous week's lesson through guided questions. Teacher should teach using participatory method to explain the two lesson outlines with relevant Bible references. He should summarise, conclude and evaluate the lesson. He should also give assignment to students from the workbook.

iii. ***TEXT REVIEW***: Genesis 18:9-14

- God's faithfulness is seen in His words. whenever He speaks, they are established/settled. Psalm 119:89
- He said to Abraham and Sarah, You will conceive and bare a son. It was so. Genesis 18:14, 21:1-3
- Christian's attitude to the unchanging word of God should graduate from laughter of unbelief to laughter of Joy and assurance. Genesis 18:12-14 and Psalm 126:2
- Our faith should transcend all forms of "doubt-laden faith" to "now-faith". Hebrews 11:1
- Our faith should grow to the level of "speak a word and my servant shall be made whole". Matt. 8:8 and "Nevertheless, at thy word I will let down the net". Luke 5:5.

Such faith brings quick testimonies and immediate miracles. Matt. 8:13

iv. ***TEACHING METHOD***

Teacher should use Lecture teaching method.

v. ***TIME MANAGEMENT***

Teacher should use the standard time for teaching two lesson outlines.

2. LESSON OUTLINES

i. ***LESSON OUTLINE A*** – THE UNCHANGEABLE GOD AND HIS WORD

God is unchangeable (Mal. 3:6a). He also upholds His integrity through His word because:

- His word is True. Jn. 17:17
- His word is Certain. Isa. 40:8; Ps. 119:89.
- His word is Pure. Prov. 30:5; Ps. 12:6
- His word is Life. Jn. 6:63
- His word is Quick and Powerful. Heb. 4:12
- His word is Yea and Amen. 2Cor. 1:20

Class Activity – Class should differentiate between the word of man and the word of God.

ii. ***LESSON OUTLINE B*** – THE TESTIMONIES OF THE INTEGRITY

- God does not change. Hebrew 13:8
- What He did He can do again. John 5:17
- Examples of God's testimonies of integrity.
- God promised to make Abraham the father of many nations and He fulfilled it. Gen. 17:4-5; Rom. 4:17.
- God spoke about the captivity of the Israelites in a strange land and their deliverance after four hundred years. Gen. 15:13; Ex. 12:40-41.
- God promised to establish the throne of David through his seeds 2Sam. 7:12-16; 1Kgs. 1:48.
- God showed to Joseph a vision of his greatness and he fulfilled it (Gen. 37:6-7; 41:39-41.
- Jesus talked about "the temple" that will be destroyed and rebuilt after three days. Jn. 2:19; 1Cor. 15:4.

3. SUMMARY

God does not change but He changes things. His word is yea and amen, 2 Corinthians 1:20. God's children must therefore learn integrity from their heavenly father and act the same way.

4. **CONCLUSION**
   God cannot be bound by His word if the terms and conditions are not fulfilled by man, 1 Sam. 2:27-30; 3:12-13.

5. **ASSIGNMENT**
   Students should study reasons why people deceive others and how to reduce or eliminate them.

LESSON 7
GOD'S EXPECTATIONS

PRAYER POINTS – Father, let all former things which do not glorify you in my life pass away. Let all things become new, in Jesus name.

PREVIOUS KNOWLEDGE – Teacher should review the previous week's lesson.

TODAY'S LESSON

1. OPENING

i. **LESSON TEXT** – Ephesians 4:17–24

ii. **MEMORY VERSE** – "Therefore if any man be in Christ, he is a new creature:old things are passed away; behold, all things are become new" 2 Corinthians 5:17

iii. **LESSON INTRODUCTION** – In our last lesson, we learnt about new life in Christ and what transpired before the new life. This week, we want to look at what God is expecting from the new man and the benefits of a new man in Christ.

TEACHER'S DIARY

i. **LESSON AIM** – To study on God's expectations from the new man.

ii. **TEACHING OBJECTIVES AND LESSON PLAN** – After the lesson, students should be able to discover God's expectations from the new man. They should be able to mention at least four benefits of a new life in Christ. To achieve these objectives, teacher should involve the students to participate actively. They should teach the two lesson outlines and give relevant examples from the Bible to buttress the points. Teacher should summarize, conclude and evaluate the lesson. Teacher should give assignment to the students.

iii. **TEXT REVIEW** – Ephesians 4:17-24

The Ways of The Gentiles (Old man).

- They walk, think and reason vain things (vanity). V.17
- Their understandings are shallow and darkened hence the possibility of constant stumbling and falling. V.18
- They are blind in hearts although they claim to see with their eyes. V.18b
- The gentiles show strong desire for sexual pleasure (Lasciviousness) and are greedy, wanting all and never satisfied. V.19.
- The gentiles are not holy. They are unlearned in the way of God. V.18-20.
- The gentiles are corrupt in their conversations and in deeds because of various lusts.

God who is just had warned the new man in the following terms:

- Do not walk like them. V.17
- Put off the old man which is corrupt, deceitful and full of lusts. V.22
- Be renewed in your thought (mind) and spirit. V.33
- Avoid "fake holiness" instead be truly holy. V.24
- Show forth the resemblance of Christ in all ways. V.25-32

i. **TEACHING METHOD** – Teacher should use participatory teaching method.

ii. **TIME MANAGEMENT** – Teacher should share the teaching time equally between the two lesson outlines.

2. LESSON OUTLINES

i. **LESSON OUTLINE A**: GOD'S EXPECTATIONS

- All new creatures must put off the old man. Matt. 9:16
- All new creatures must put on the new man. Matt. 9:17
- New creatures must disengage from every relationship with the kingdoms of the devil. 2 Cor. 6:1-18; Eph. 5:11-12;
- New creatures must purify their thoughts and be pure in their hearts, 1 Cor. 3:16-17; Rom. 12:1-2.
- They must have regular fellowship with God. James 4:8; 1 John 1:1-3
- They must have regular fellowship with brethren. Heb. 10:25, Acts 2:42-47.
- They must act in faith and please God always. Heb. 11:6

CLASS ACTIVITY 1 – Class should discuss how God would probably feel if He sees the new creatures behaving differently from His divine expectation.

i. ***LESSON OUTLINE B*** – BENEFITS OF A NEW LIFE IN CHRIST.
- The new man becomes joint-heirs with Christ. Romans 8:16-17.
- The new man will be able to do all Christ did while here on earth. John 14:12a.
- The new man will do greater work that Christ did. John 14:12b.
- The new man will enjoy everlasting life. John 3:16; John 17:3
- The new man will enjoy benefits of righteousness. 1 Peters 2:24.
- Restoration to life raise the dead. Acts 4:39-41; deep knowledge, wisdom and unparalleled understanding. Acts 14:13.
- Blessing of riches. 2 Cor. 8:9; Sound health, fruitfulness joy, beauty, glory, etc. Isaiah 63:1-3

3. **SUMMARY**

God expects all old man to put off their old nature and put on a new man after Christ. Those who put on a new man through genuine repentance have a lot of benefits awaiting them. Those who refuse to be transformed would be punished severely for their defiance.

4. CONCLUSION

God expects much from those who have new life in Christ. It is high time you began to manifest the new life and enjoy the benefits.

1. ASSIGNMENT

Class should identify factors which can make the new man behave in the old ways and suggest solution to this anomaly

LESSON 8
GOD IS COMMITTED TO MAN

PRAYER POINT — Pray that the Lord will open your eyes of understanding and grant you the grace to be committed to the Lord

PREVIOUS KNOWLEDGE — The teacher should ask the students what it means to be committed to each other in the area of employment as it relates to payment for work done and promotion.

TODAY'S LESSON

1. OPENING

   i. ***TEXT*** – 1 Timothy 6:11-21

   ii. ***MEMORY VERSE*** – "And I will very gladly spend and be spent for your souls; though the more abundantly I love you, the less I am loved" 2 Corinthians 12:15

   iii. ***LESSON INTRODUCTION*** – The success or otherwise of any project depends to the level of commitment. Commitment to the Almighty God is the highest priority for the Christian and it cannot be taken lightly because of its eternal implications. It also makes the difference between acceptance and blessing or disapproval and divine wrath. Luke 9:62. The wife of love was not willing to commit to obeying the instructions of God; she looked back and became a pillar of salt. She exchanged warm, living, vibrant flesh for an inanimate, unfeeling, physical pillar of salt. Genesis 19:26. The lack of commitment that began with her husband affected her, and spread to their offspring who committed incest with their father.

TEACHER'S DIARY

   i. ***LESSON AIM*** – To study commitment to the Lord

ii. ***TEACHING OBJECTIVES AND LESSON PLAN*** – At the end of this study, students should be able to tell in what areas God is committed to man and what areas of man should be committed to God.

iii. ***TEXT REVIEW*** – 1 Timothy 6:11-21
   - God wants us to be committed to righteousness, godliness, faith, love patience and meekness – vs. 11
   - Personal efforts are required to be committed; here it is to flee – vs. 11
   - Commitment requires some fighting, though a good fight to get to eternal life – vs. 12
   - The call to commitment requires us and the witnesses are God and Jesus Christ – vs. 13
   - We should be committed till the second coming of Christ which is at hand – vs. 14
   - Our commitment should be fervent because no one except God know when Christ will come – vs.15
   - It is not wise to be committed to riches because wealth is not reliable – vs. 17
   - We should be committed to God who gives and can sustains wealth – vs. 17
   - Wealth should be spent to do good works and be spent to bless others – vs. 18
   - This is the best way to sustain whatever riches God has given – vs. 19
   - Personal efforts are necessary to keep what is committed unto our hands by God – vs. 20
   - Commitment does not allow for unnecessary and unfruitful talks – vs. 21
   - It is necessary to guide the tongue if we are to be committed to the end – vs. 21

iv. ***TEACHING METHOD*** – We recommend discussion with some lecture methods.

v. ***TIME MANAGEMENT*** – Go straight to your points and avoid unnecessary class distractions.

2. LESSON OUTLINES

i. ***LESSON OUTLINE A*** – GOD IS TOTALLY COMMITTED TO MAN
   - Jesus Christ was declared as the slain Lamb of God before the foundation of the earth – John 1:29; Revelation 3:8
   - Jesus was to redeem and reconcile man to God – 1 John 3:5
   - He was to pay completely for the consequences of the disobedience and rebellion of man – Hebrews 2:9
   - Jesus Christ had to go through the cross of Calvary – Galatians 3:13
   - He went through unimaginable agony, humiliation and pain for the sake of man – Matthew 26:67-68; 27:26-46; Isaiah 53:7; 1 Peter 3:18; 1 Corinthians 5:7; Titus 2:14
   - He had to remake us and we became kings and priests unto our God – Revelation 1:5-6; Galatians 1:4; Ephesians 5:2
   - God is committed to us twenty-four-seven in all places, and in all circumstance.
   - He is fully committed to our prosperity – Deuteronomy 8:18, 2 Corinthians 8:9
   - He is committed to our Health. Isaiah 53:5; Luke 4:18; Matthew 8:17; 1 Peter 2:24
   - He is committed to our Physical Protection Psalm 125:2; Psalm 27:1-3
   - He is committed to our matrimonial success Eph. 5:22-33.
   - He is committed to our academic success, Deuteronomy 28:13; James 1:5.

ii. ***LESSON OUTLINE B*** – WE NEED TO RECIPROCATE GOD'S COMMITMENT

- He commands in His word, that all we are must be dedicated to loving him. Mark 12:30.
- Other things will take over the life of a man who is not totally committed to God – Illustrate this with the life of Solomon – 1 Kings 3:11-13, 1 Kings 4:20-34, 1 Kings 10:1-10, 1 Kings 11:1-14, 23-25, 26-35.
- God is looking for those who will make Him the first in all things in their lives – 2 Chr. 16:9a
- If you decide to be committed God will give grace to be humble, to forgive offences, to be free from the love of money, to serve others, not boss them, to accept rebuke and to persevere – 1 Peter 5:5-6; Matthew 18:32-35; Mark 9:35; Mark 10:42-45.

3. SUMMARY

God is totally committed to man and there is no justification if man does not respond completely. God is looking for those who make Him the first and most important person in their lives and the result could be great.

4. CONCLUSION

There is no excuse for lack of total commitment to God

5. ASSIGNMENT

Let the students study the result of commitment to God at the present age and in the life to come.

LESSON 9
VESSELS UNTO HONOR

PRAYER POINT – Father, let me remain (or become) vessel unto honor for the rest of my life, in Jesus name.

PREVIOUS KNOWLEDGE – Teacher should review last week's lesson by asking guided questions from the students on the memory verse, the lesson outlines, summary and conclusion.

TODAY'S LESSON

1. OPENING

　i. **LESSON TEXT** – 2 Timothy 2:19-21

　ii. **MEMORY VERSE** – "Nevertheless the foundation of God standeth sure, having this seal, The Lord knoweth them that are his. And, Let every one that nameth the name of Christ depart from iniquity" 2 Timothy 2:19

　iii. **LESSON INTRODUCTION** – God is absolutely pure and desires that His children be of the same quality too, 1 Pet. 1:15-16; Matt. 5:48. The Almighty God cannot compromise this standard if He has to find a pure vessel to use. 2 Tim. 2:19.

TEACHER'S DIARY

　i. **LESSON AIM** – To study the actual meaning and qualities of vessel unto honor.

　ii. **TEACHING OBJECTIVES AND LESSON PLAN** – Through the lesson, students should be able to explain the actual meaning of vessel unto honor. They should be able to mention at least five qualities of vessel unto honor. To achieve these objectives teacher should teach the two lesson outline, summarize, conclude and evaluate the lesson. However, students should be actively involved. Teacher should give assignment.

iii. ***TEXT REVIEW*** – 2 Timothy 2:19-21

The instructions for the vessel unto honor to remain honorable unto God include the following:
- Depart from iniquity, 2 Tim. 2:19
- Purge yourself of these dishonorable elements, i. e. contaminators. vs. 21
- Flee lusts, vs. 22
- Avoid foolish and unlearned questions vs. 23.
- Do not strive. vs. 24

The vessels unto honor were encouraged to imbibe the following attitudes:
- Be sanctified, vs. 21
- Be Prepared for every good work, vs. 21
- Follow righteousness, faith charity and peace. vs. 22
- Be gentle, teachable and patient. vs. 24
- Show meekness to all men to save same from the devil. vs. 25-26

iv. ***TEACHING METHOD*** – Teacher should use the lecture and discussion teaching method.

v. ***TIME MANAGEMENT*** – Teacher should use the standard time for teaching two lesson outlines.

2. LESSON OUTLINES

i. ***LESSON OUTLINE A*** – VESSEL UNTO HONOUR DEFINED

What is the vessel unto honor?
- They are believers who are separated unto the Lord Jesus Christ for every good work. 2 Tim 2:21.
- They are sanctified believers, 1 Tim. 2:21

- They are holy believers who are perfect like their father in heaven, 1 Peters 1:15-16; Matt. 5:48.
- The devil could not find any fault in Jesus because he was a vessel unto honor to God. John 14:30.

Class Activity – Class should discuss how a believer can become a vessel unto honor.

ii. *LESSON OUTLINE B* – THEIR QUALITIES

Vessels unto honor should possess the following qualities:
- Cleanliness - All round clean without blemish, Dan. 1:8, 18
- Holiness - Mortify the deeds of the flesh, Col. 3:5; Gal. 5:10-21; Romans 12:9
- Submission- To God and for God in everything. James 4:7
- Denial-Refusal to be engrossed with the worldly pleasure, 1 John 2:15-17; I Tim. 6:10.
- Prayerfulness-Consistence in prayer. Matthew 26:37-41.

iii. Studious-Life devoted to the studying of the word of God, 2 Tim. 2:15.
- Evangelism- They must be an incurable soul winner, John 15:1-7.
- Powerful- They are filled with the power of the Holy Spirit, Act 1:8
- Reliance- They rely absolutely on the Holy Spirit for direction, John 14:2b; John 15:26

3. SUMMARY
Vessel unto honor are sanctified believers who are prepared unto every good work. They possess certain qualities which include prayerfulness, holiness, devotion, etc. They have duties which are enabled by the power of the Holy Spirit.

4. CONCLUSION
The Lord Jesus is desperately in search of vessels unto honor, hence He spent His first earthly sojourn not only to recruit, but also to train, sanc-

tify, disciple and commission those He found. May He find in us vessels unto honor in Jesus name.

5. **ASSIGNMENT**
Students should study the expected duties of the vessel unto honor.

LESSON 10
GOD'S NATURE AND EXPECTATION

PRAYER POINT – Father, help me to be holy for you for the rest of my life in Jesus name.

PREVIOUS KNOWLEDGE – Teacher should allow students to review the previous week's lesson through guided questions.

TODAY'S LESSON

1. OPENING

   i. ***LESSON TEXT*** – Leviticus 19:1-4

   ii. ***MEMORY VERSE*** – "Speak unto all the congregation of the children of Israel, and say unto them, Ye shall be holy: for I the LORD your God am holy". Leviticus 19:2

   iii. ***LESSON INTRODUCTION*** – God is holy in an excellent, infinitely perfect and incomparable manner. Isa.6:3, Exo.15:11. Holiness denotes the very essence of God. God is the fountain of holiness, innocence, and sanctification. He created man in His own image and likeness. Gen.1:26. In this lesson, we shall be studying holiness as the nature of God and His expectation from mankind.

TEACHER'S DIARY

   i. ***LESSON AIM*** – To study the holy nature of God.

   ii. ***TEACHING OBJECTIVES AND LESSON PLAN*** – After the lesson, students should be able to understand that holiness is the nature of God and discover that God places high expectation on the need for man to be holy. Students should take the opening prayer, review the last week lesson, read the Bible Passage, recite the memory verse and do the class activities.

iii. ***TEXT REVIEW***: Leviticus 19:1-4
- God commanded all His children to be holy- Leviticus 19:2.
- God gave directives to His children to avoid certain avenues which will lead to pollution of their holiness. These are:
- The path of idols. V.4
- Unwilling offering. V.5
- Unholy meal. V.5
- Neglect of the poor/stranger. V.9-10
- Avoid stealing, falsehood, lies, cheating, robbery, oppressing the physically challenged, hatred, vengeance, etc. V.12-18
- God commanded all His children to be righteous in all their dealings and in judgment. V.15

iv. ***TEACHING METHOD*** – Teacher should combine the lecture, question and answer teaching methods.

v. ***TIME MANAGEMENT*** – Teacher should share the teaching time between two lesson outlines.

2. LESSON OUTLINES

i. LESSON OUTLINES A – HOLINESS IS THE NATURE OF GOD
- God is holy in nature: Exodus 15:1
- The throne of God is holy. Psalm 47:8
- The habitation of God is holy. Isaiah 63:15, Psalm 93:5.
- The court of God is holy. Isaiah 62:9
- His angels are holy. Revelation 14:10
- His works are holy. Psalm 145:17
- God is holy in Character. Psalm 22:3

- The name of the Lord is holy. Isaiah 57:15a.
- His words are Holy. Jeremiah 23:9
- His sanctuary is holy. I Chronicle 16:29

CLASS ACTIVITY 1 – What are the reasons why God will not tolerate unholy things in His presence?

ii. ***LESSON OUTLINE B*** – GOD'S EXPECTATIONS FROM MANKIND
- God commands His children to be holy. Lev. 11:44; I Pet. 1:15
- God called His children holy people. I Peters 2:9
- They should praise and reverence Him in Holiness. Psalm 30:4; Rev.15:4
- Their thoughts and actions should conform to the holy nature of God. Romans 6:19; 12:2; Eph. 1:4
- Their services and worship must be holy. Joshua 24:19

3. SUMMARY
God is holy and unholy life must be avoided in its totality. Believers must be holy.

4. CONCLUSION
Although mankind lost all holiness in the fall (Rom.6:23), God makes His people gradually "partakers of His holiness" here on earth as they surrender their lives to His saving grace and lordship through Jesus Christ. And in heaven, they will be found perfectly and forever sanctified. You too can be holy.

5. ASSIGNMENT
Students should identify enemies of holiness and discuss how believers can overcome them.

LESSON 11
KING ASA WAS RIGHTEOUS

PRAYER POINT – Pray that God will use them to make a difference in their generation, also pray that God should pull down all altars of idols in the land of America.

PREVIOUS KNOWLEDGE – Class teacher should remind the students of that coming to God's presence with a proud and arrogant heart makes ones' worship unacceptable to God, also a humble contrite and thankful heart will be rewarded.

TODAY'S LESSON

1. **OPENING**

    i. ***LESSON TEXT*** – 1 Kings 15:9-24, 2 Chr. 14:2

    ii. ***MEMORY VERSE*** – "Asa did what was right in the eyes of the Lord, as his father David had done" 1 Kings 15:11

    iii. ***LESSON INTRODUCTION*** – The kingdom of Israel divided into two after King Solomon died. Jeroboam was in the southern part called Israel while Rehoboam, Solomon's son ruled in the Northern part called Judah. His reign was evil for 17 years (1 Kgs. 14:21). His son Abijam reigned for few years because he was evil (31/2 years) 1 Kgs. 15:1-2. After Abijah, his son Asa became king in Judah. Asa ruled for 35 years peacefully. God blessed, protected and prospered his reign. It was recorded that Asa did what was good and right in the eyes of the Lord his God. 1 Kg. 15:11. In this study we shall discuss what King Asa did and the various lessons we can learn from his life.

TEACHER'S DIARY

i. ***LESSON AIM*** – To learn how righteous leadership exhausts and prospers a nation.

ii. ***TEACHING OBJECTIVES AND LESSON PLAN*** – At the end of the lesson, students should be able to understand that idolatry is abomination to God, righteousness is rewarding, a Christian must be separate and come out of iniquities. To achieve these objectives, teacher should explain both outlines as stated in the teacher's manual.

iii. ***TEXT REVIEW***:1 Kings 15:9-24, 2 Chr. 14:2
  - Asa became king in Judah in the 20th year reign of Jeroboam as king in Israel. Vs 9
  - He had a long reign (41yrs) unlike his predecessors. Vs 10
  - He worshiped God like King David and it was right before God. Vs 11
  - He did not worship idols like his predecessors, but stopped Idol worshiping and prostitution from the land. Vs 12
  - He dethroned his grandmother's (Maakah) and destroyed hers idols. Vs 13.
  - He gave and committed his heart to God completely. Vs 14

iv. ***TEACHING METHOD*** – Teacher should use discussion method.

v. ***TIME MANAGEMENT*** – Teacher should share teaching time equally between the two lesson outlines.

2. LESSON OUTLINES

i. ***LESSON OUTLINE A*** – ASA'S BACKGROUND – 1 KINGS 15:9-10
  - Asa's father and grandfathers were idols worshipers. 1Kgs 15:3; Ex 20:1-5; Lev 26:1; Ezk 14:3,

- Asa's grandmother, Maacah who brought him up was an idolatress. This Shows, that his grandfather, his father and grandmother were evil. Ps 115:4-8
- People of the land lived in unrighteousness and evil by building high places and groves for idol worship, Lev 26:1
- The land was filled with sodomites (homosexual) and prostitutes which were abominations before God, 1 Kg. 14:22-24.
- Despite the fact that Asa up bring was among idol worshipers, he chose to serve the living God of Abraham, Isaac and Jacob.

CLASS ACTIVITY – Ephesians 5:20 – Class should review this passage

ii. ***LESSON OUTLINE B*** – ASA'S REIGN. 1 Kgs 15:11-13

- He lived a righteous life and carried out a religious reform in the whole land of Judah. Dan 3:8
- He established a just government. There was a record of him that "Asa did which was right in the eyes of the Lord, as did David his father." 1 Kg 15:11.
- Asa's reigned peacefully for 35years.
- What a credit comparing Asa to David. Think of David's fervency and sincerity to God.

Asa's moral reform included the following:

- An end to religious prostitution in the land (Homosexual). Lev 18:22, Rom 1:26-27
- Sexual ritual was forbidden throughout the land. 1 Kg 14:24 compared to 1 Kings 15:12. Col 3:15
- Asa started his charity from this home by removing all the idols his forefathers had made 1 Kg 15:12.
- He removed his grandmother Maacah from her position as queen mother. 1Kg 15:12-13 because she had made an idol in a grove.
- This is a serious height of commitment to God and not man. He loved the Lord more than idolatry in his family or in all the land. Think of the family implications.
- He was ready to cleanse the land of idolatry no matter whose ox was gored.

How does this affect the respect for elders as it relates to Asa?
- It was recorded that Asa did not remove the high places. It must however be noted that there were high places where the Lord was the focus of worship 1 Kg. 3:2; 1 Sam. 9:12. We can conclude that high places for idol worship were destroyed while those where the true God was worshipped were allowed to remain.
- Asa dedicated silver gold and vessels consecrated by his father. Dedicating things which his father had dedicated could be a form of retribution 1Kg. 15:15.

3. SUMMARY
Asa was the instrument God used to save the nation of Judah because he was righteous and his heart was total committed to God.

2. CONCLUSION
The name Asa means "healing." The people of Judah were diseased with idolatry, which was "detestable" in the Lord's sight. Asa brought healing to Judah by both destroying the idols and by repairing the altar of the Lord. One of the reasons God has called you, planted you in your family, school, and amongst your current brothers, sisters, and everyone is that you should make a difference. Will you disappoint God? The choice is yours.

3. ASSIGNMENT
Make this lesson applicable to your life by asking yourself this simple question, am I righteous?

LESSON 12
DESTINY – DEFINITION OF DISCOVERY

PRAYER POINT – Father, help me to identify and fulfill my specific destinies, in Jesus name.

PREVIOUS KNOWLEDGE – Students should review the previous week's lesson with attention on

the memory verse and the two lesson outlines.

TODAY'S LESSON

1. OPENING

i. ***LESSON TEXT*** – Jeremiah 1:4-7

ii. ***MEMORY VERSE*** – "And the LORD answered me, and said, write the vision, and make it plain upon tables, that he may run that readeth it" Habakkuk 2:2.

iii. ***LESSON INTRODUCTION*** – Destiny can be broadly categorized into two groups. The first category is the general destiny which is an expression of God's thought for all of mankind. Jn 3:16; 2 Pet.3:9. Every believer is to be His ambassador. 2 Cor.5:20-21 and to prosper spiritually and physically 3 Jn.2. God however has specific destinies for some individuals; this is a divine assignment/purpose for which such people have been created. Acts 26:15-18, Jer.1:5.

TEACHER'S DIARY

i. ***LESSON AIM*** – To study the meaning of destiny and how it can be recovered.

ii. ***TEACHING OBJECTIVES AND LESSON PLAN*** – After the lesson, students should be able to define destiny or understand the meaning of destiny and discover the categories of destiny. Teacher should allow students to take the opening prayer, recite the memory verse and thereafter read the Bible Passage. They should also do the two class activities. Teacher should allow the Assistant Teacher to conduct the class and assist the students in the class activities, should teach the two lesson outlines, summarize, conclude and evaluate the lesson. Teacher should give assignment to students from the workbook.

iii. ***TEXT REVIEW***:Jeremiah 1:4-7

The role of God as the ultimate owner of our beings are stated in the following terms in Jeremiah 1:5

- I formed you.
- I knew you.
- I sanctified you.
- I ordained you a prophet.
- Say not I am a child.
- Thou will speak whatever I command you.
- Be not afraid of their faces.
- I am with you to deliver you.
- I have put my word in your mouth.
- I have set you over nations and kingdoms.

What a creator and owner who knows us when we had not any existence and absolute nothing! Now that we have become something from nothing and somebody from nobody, we should live for the one who raised us from nothing and who could return us to nothing. Jeremiah 32:17, 27

i. ***TEACHING METHOD*** – Teacher should use combined question and answer and lecture teaching method.

ii. ***TIME MANAGEMENT*** – Teacher should use the standard time teaching two lesson outlines.

2. LESSON OUTLINES

i. *LESSON OUTLINE A* – DESTINY DEFINED
- Destiny is the purpose of God for man's life.
- Destiny is a divinely pre-planned destination and designation in life. Jer. 1:15.
- Destiny is the totality of God's counsel for a man.
- Destiny is what God has decided concerning man before he/she was conceived. Isaiah 25:1; 49:1, Eph. 1:4
- God stated that the destiny of the Lord Jesus was to save His people from their sins. Matt. 1:21; John 18:37
- God's destiny for man is great, to give him an expected end. Jeremiah 29:1
- God destined greatness for Abraham. Gen 18:17-18.
- God destined that Samson would divinely deliver the Israelites from the Philistines. Judges 13:5
- Our attitudes to God affect the attainment or otherwise of our destinies. John 15:5; Judges 16:30;

CLASS ACTIVITY – Identify and discuss desirable attitudes to attain our destinies.

ii. *LESSON OUTLINE 2* – DESTINY DISCOVERED
- It is important to discover your destiny for you to recover and fulfill it.
- Destiny can be discovered through the following means:
- Through prayerful enquiring from the Lord. Eph. 1:17-21, Matt 7:7-9;
- Through revelation by the Holy Spirit who bears witness for us. Acts 13:1-4, Rom 8:14, Act 7:22-25
- Through angelic revelation/visitation. Judges 6:11-14, 13:2-5; Matt. 1:26-31
- Through revelation in dreams from God. Gen. 37:5-10. Through observation of trend, patterns, passions, interest, etc. Genesis 37:11; Luke 1:66; Luke 2:19.

CLASS ACTIVITY 2 – The devil has evil intentions, plans and purpose for human beings. How can these plans be aborted or changed?

3. **SUMMARY**
   Destiny can be discovered and recovered also. It can also be discovered through intense prayer, inspiration by the Holy Spirit, and others.

4. **CONCLUSION**
   Seek the face of God, lift up your faith unto God and run with the vision which the Lord will give to you. God will always be there to back you up Ps.139:14-17.

5. **ASSIGNMENT**
   Students should study how the intentions and plans of the devil can be aborted or changed.

Lesson 13

THE FIRST QUARTER INTERACTIVE SESSION

Welcome to the first interactive session!

Your privilege:

- To ask questions on treated lessons for clarity
- To give critical appraisal of the outline
- To give useful suggestions towards better performance
- To give useful spiritual contributions

LESSON 14
ENEMIES OF DESTINY

PRAYER POINT – Father, deliver me from any attitude capable of destroying my destiny, in Jesus name.

PREVIOUS KNOWLEDGE – Teacher should review the previous week's lesson.

TODAY'S LESSON

1. OPENING

   i. ***LESSON TEXT*** – 2 Timothy 3:1-7

   ii. ***MEMORY VERSE*** – "He that hath clean hands, and a pure heart; who hath not lifted up his soul unto vanity, nor sworn deceitfully". Psalm 24:4

   iii. ***LESSON INTRODUCTION*** – We were able to discover in our last lesson that destiny could be general or specific. It is the thought and plan of God for us that we must discover and fulfill. Today, we shall examine some destiny destroyers with a view to avoiding them in our lives.

TEACHER'S DIARY

   i. ***LESSON AIM*** – The study aims at discovering the enemies of destiny.

   ii. ***TEACHING OBJECTIVES AND LESSON PLAN*** – Through the lesson, students should be able to discover some enemies of destinies. Teacher should allow the students to take the opening prayer together, then recite memory verse and read the Bible Passage.

   iii. ***TEXT REVIEW*** – 2 Timothy 3:1-7

All the elements of perilous time are enemies of destiny. They must be identified by the individual and be dealt with through the power of our Lord Jesus Christ. The elements are: Self-lovers, Covetousness, Boasting, Pride, Blasphemy, Disobedience to parents, Ingrate, Unholy, Unaffectionate, Trucebreaker, False accusers, Incontinent, Fierce, Despisers of good things, Traitors, Heady, High mindedness, Lovers of pleasure, Fake Christian.

Those who possess these traits or are guilty of the crime so identified, really have to seek the face of God for deliverance and forgiveness or else, they will not get to their goals (they shall proceed no further). II Tim. 3:9

iv. ***TEACHING METHOD*** – Teacher should use the lecture teaching method.

v. ***TIME MANAGEMENT*** – Teacher should share the teaching time between the two lesson outlines.

2. LESSON OUTLINES

i. ***LESSON OUTLINE B*** – SOME ENEMIES OF DESTINY.

The under listed items are the enemies of destiny:

- Sin - A sinner who refuses to confess his/her sin can never fulfill God's plan for his/her life. Roman 3:23, Proverbs 14:34; Psalm 7:11, Judges 16:6-18
- Prayerlessness - A Christian who avoids night vigil, prayer meetings (home or church) can never fulfill destiny. Luke 18:1; Matt 26:38-42.
- Pride- The proud would be resisted by God and therefore cannot fulfill destiny. Psalm 138:6, James 4:6; Dan. 4:28-33.
- Secularity - A fellow who pursues mundane or vain glory or vanity and excessive desires for wealth can never fulfill destiny. Ecc. 2:10-11; I Kings 11:1-10.
- Ignorance - Those who lack the knowledge or ability of God or the knowledge of the Holy Spirit can never fulfill destiny. Hosea 4:6; Prov. 29:18; I Cor. 2:10; Rom. 8:26-27

CLASS ACTIVITY – Discuss how believers can overcome or defeat enemies of destiny.

   ii. ***LESSON OUTLINE B*** – MORE ENEMIES TO DEFEAT

      The enemies so identified hereunder are also destiny destroyers. To fulfill destiny, they must be destroyed:

- Doubt and faithlessness: Those who do not believe God or lack faith in His word will never fulfill destiny. Heb. 4:2; I Tim. 1:19; James 1:6-8; Numbers 14:22-24; Matthew 17:19-22
- Laziness- Lazy, idle and indolent persons can never fulfill destiny- John 4:31-34; Prov. 18:9; 16; Proverb 22:29; John 5:17; John 9:4.
- Demonic Attacks- Those who are under demonic influences, demonic attack, satanic captivity and bondage can never fulfill destiny- Eph. 6:12; Dan.10:12-13; John 10:10; Exodus 15:9.

3. SUMMARY

All enemies of destiny must first be destroyed before one can fulfill destiny and Jesus can handle their defeat with your cooperation.

4. CONCLUSION

Divine destiny has a lot of enemies working against its fulfillment. Every child of God must fight the good fight of faith against these identified enemies daily. 1 Tim. 6:12.

5. ASSIGNMENT

Can a lazy fellow or a liar fulfill destiny? Divide the students into two groups. A group to study the lazy fellow and the other group to study the liar in the area of destiny.

LESSON 15
RECOVER YOUR DESTINY

PRAYER POINT – Father, let me recover my lost destiny, in Jesus name.

PREVIOUS KNOWLEDGE – Teacher should comment on the Quarterly Review exercise in term of participation and performance. Teacher should encourage students to attain better performance in the 2nd quarter of the Sunday School.

TODAY'S LESSON

1. OPENING

i. **LESSON TEXT** – Habakkuk 2:1-4

ii. **MEMORY VERSE** – "I will stand upon my watch, and set me upon the tower, and will watch to see what he will say unto me, and what I shall answer when I am reproved". Habakkuk 2:1

iii. **LESSON INTRODUCTION** – In our last two lessons, we identified what destiny is and how we can discover it. We also took time to identify the destroyers of destiny; in this lesson we shall be looking at how some people lost their destinies and how to recover divine destiny.

TEACHER'S DIARY

i. **LESSON AIM**: To study how to recover destiny.

ii. **TEACHING OBJECTIVES AND TEACHING PLAN** – At the end of the lesson, students should be able to understand how destiny can be recovered. Teacher should allow the students to take the opening prayer, read the Bible Passage, recite the memory verse and do the two class activities. Assistant Teacher to do the lesson introduction and lead the class in the two class activities, teach the lesson outlines with the relevant Bible reference then summaries, conclude and evaluate the lesson. Teacher should give assignment to the students from the work book.

iii. ***TEXT REVIEW*** – Habakkuk 2:1-4

Having kept transgression at bay, Habakkuk 2:5, then "living by faith" is one of the ways to fulfill destiny. Habakkuk 2:4. Destiny race is like a vision which one sees at a distance. The end of each person's destiny varies just as our life's plan varies, but running by that vision would help to keep within the track and ambit of the race rule. Therefore, Prophet Habakkuk provided the following guides (Hab.2:1-5):

- Write down the revealed destiny upon readable platform.
- Run by it as you read it.
- Understand that every day is a time component of the destiny race.
- Note that the fulfillment time may not be now, but cannot be at infinity or endless.
- Understand that God's-given destiny will surely come to pass.
- Live by faith.
- Avoid unrighteous living, cutting corners and pride.
- Then, you will get there one day, surely soon.

iv. ***TEACHING METHOD*** – Teacher should use lecture teaching method.

v. ***TIME MANAGEMENT*** – Teacher should use the standard time for teaching two lesson outlines.

2. LESSON OUTLINES

i. ***LESSON OUTLINE A*** – LOST DESTINIES

There are instances of lost destinies in the Bible. For instance:
- Eli's family lost the priesthood destiny due to the wayward lifestyle of his children, Hophni and Phinehas. I Sam. 2:27-30.

- Gehazi lost his prophetic destiny due to covetousness. 2nd Kings 5:20-27
- Judas Iscariot lost the Apostolic destiny due to greed and iniquity. Matt. 27:3-5; and Acts 1:16-18.
- Samson lost the destiny of delivering the Israelites from the Philistines due to lust after strange women. Judges 16:6-7; 20-23;
- Vashti lost her destiny to remain the queen due to her arrogance. Esther 1:10-19
- Demas lost the destiny in the kingdom race due to love of the world. 2 Tim. 4:10.

CLASS ACTIVITY – Class should identify those factors that can cause someone to lose destiny according to 1 Cor. 6:9-11

ii. ***LESSON OUTLINE B*** – RECOVERING DESTINY

Destiny can be recovered by the following methods:
- Offensive attack to the kingdom of darkness and satanic work against our destiny. Eph. 6:12-18; I Thess. 5:17-18.
- Hard work as means of defeating laziness and idleness. Eph. 5:14-16; Prv. 10:4; Ecc. 9:10.
- Build up your faith: become a bible addict. Rom.10:17, Col.3:16, Jos.1:8.
- Destroy ignorance of God's word, will and purpose. Jer. 29:11-14; Ps 119:105, 130.
- Eliminate pride in all areas of your life. Jam.4:6-10
- Seek the kingdom of the Almighty God and not the vanity of the world. Matt.6:33; Heb.12:1-2; Rom 12:1-2.
- Intensify your prayer life. Lk. 18:1, Jn.16:24.
- Flee from every form or appearance of sin. Isa.59:1-2, 1 Thess.5:22.

3. **SUMMARY**

Destiny could be lost, lost destiny could be recovered through the Holy instruments of spiritual war-fare and holiness. God has blessed and will bless people who are faithful to their callings.

4. **CONCLUSION**

    It is time to rise up and take up the path of your divine destiny so that at Christ's appearing which could be at any time, you will not be ashamed

5. **ASSIGNMENT**

    Can destiny be lost? Students should study how somebody could recover lost destiny if they support that it could be lost or explain if they believe it cannot be lost.

LESSON 16
EARTHLY CITIZENSHIP

PRAYER POINT – Ask that the Almighty God grant all students divine wisdom and insight into the Word of God today. Pray that the wisdom of God revealed today will be translated into godly action.

PREVIOUS KNOWLEDGE – Teacher to review the previous week's lesson.

TODAY'S LESSON

1. OPENING

i. ***LESSON TEXT*** – Romans 13:1-10

ii. ***MEMORY VERSE*** – "Let every soul be subject to the governing authorities. For there is no authority except from God, and the authorities that exist are appointed by God," Romans 13:1

iii. ***LESSON INTRODUCTION*** – The privilege of belonging to a city or country is defined as citizenship. It is also the state of being vested with the rights, privileges, and duties of a citizen. We live here on earth and are citizens of different countries and nations. Children of God are citizens of heaven, Phil. 4:20, and are on earth as the salt of the earth. Some are dual citizens of several countries even on earth. An obedient Christian must be a good citizen of heaven and earth. The Christian faith demands responsible citizenship. Democracy, by its very nature, requires citizen participation in the processes of government at every level—local, state, and national. God expects every Christian of mature age to play his / her part. God's people must be concerned not only about the world to come but also about the world in which we presently live.

TEACHER'S DIARY

i. ***LESSON AIM*** – To challenge students to rise up as responsible citizens and contribute meaningfully to the society and nation that they belong to.

ii. ***TEACHING OBJECTIVES AND LESSON PLAN*** – At the end of the lesson, students should be enlightened about the Biblical requirements of their civic responsibilities to their earthly country of citizenship. Students should be able to mention at least four privileges of Christians to their earthly countries. They should be able to enumerate at least four responsibilities of a Christian citizen of an earthly country. These should ultimately lead to a change in attitude and commitment to the society that they belong to. To achieve these objectives, the teacher should.

iii. ***TEXT REVIEW*** – Romans 13:1-10

We can learn from the text of today the following:

- Every soul must obey any government in authority because no one gets to any position except it is ordained of God, vs. 1; Titus 3:1; 1 Pet. 2:13-14.
- Anyone who resists authority, resists the ordinances of God, vs. 2; 1 Chr. 29:23; 2 Chr. 8:15; Eccl. 8:2; Ezra 7:26.
- Rulers are expected to be just, vs. 3; 2 Sam. 23:3
- A major reason to be subject is for the sake of conscience, vs. 5; Acts 23:1; Heb. 10:22.
- We must pay taxes, vs. 6; Luke 20:22-23.
- Do unto others what you want them to do unto you including expressions of love, vs. 8; Matt. 7:12; 1 Cor. 8:21.
- The summary of all commandments is to love your neighbor as yourself, vs. 9; 1 Thess. 3:12; 2 Jn. 1:5.
- Love is all, vs. 10; 1 Cor. 13:1, 13.

iv. ***TEACHING METHOD*** – Use discussion method.

v. **TIME MANAGEMENT** – Teacher should allocate time equally to the two lesson outlines.

2. LESSON OUTLINES

i. ***LESSON OUTLINE A*** – RIGHTS / PRIVILEGES
- Citizen by birth Ps.87:4-5, Acts 22:27-28, Acts 23:27 Different nations have constitutional laws on citizenship by birth
- Passport Ne. 2:5-7 A passport identifies you as part of a citizen of a nation.
- Vote or put worthy people in place Job 34:18, Prov. 25:19, Ex. 32:25-35. This is both a right/privilege and a duty! This topic will be discussed fuller in the coming week.
- Freedom of speech Acts 21:37-40, Rm. 9:1-5 Speak the truth Mat. 5:14-16, 1 Cor. 15:34, Ps. 94:16. Are you a 'politically correct' Christian when you speak?
- Justice Lk. 18:2-5, Mic. 6:8, Esth. 6:1-3, Is. 1:17

ii. ***LESSON OUTLINE B*** – DUTIES / RESPONSIBILITIES
- Obey the laws, authority Rm. 13:1-3, 1 Pet. 2:13-14, Tit. 3:1, Ez. 7:26
- Work, improve the economy Lk. 19:12-13, Ecc. 2:3-6, Prov. 10:4, Pov. 12:24, Ecc. 9:10 A lazy Christian living off government handouts is a shame to the gospel.
- Pay taxes Mk. 12:13-17, Rm. 13:7 It is ungodly to willfully scam the government on your taxes. Are you an honest tax-paying citizen?
- Pray for those in authority Ez. 6:10, 1 Tim. 2:1-2, Jer. 29:7, 2 Chr. 7:14, Ps. 122:6-7. This is so important and an excuse that the leaders or situation is bad is untenable. Abraham interceded for the cities of Sodom and Gomorrah (Gen. 18:23-33), so did Moses for the nation of Israel in its infancy (Ex. 32:11). Apostle Paul encouraged Christians to "pray for the emperor" even though that emperor was a mad tyrant like Nero (1 Tim. 2:1-2). There is no nation, continent, city or people on earth that can keep the power of intercession out.

- Patriotic Es. 2:21-23, 2 Sam. 20:2, Is. 62:1, 2 Sam. 11:11, 2 Kgs. 7:9, Neh. 2:3. Loyalty and patriotism must not be at the expense of our Christian faith.

3. **SUMMARY**
A Christian is primarily a dual citizen – of heaven and of an earthly nation. All Christians must meet the requirements of both locations.

4. **CONCLUSION**
It is important to consider your citizenship here on earth as a day of reckoning will come. Can your citizenship be described as Christian? Put into practice all that you have learnt today and make a difference in your nation. Let your citizenship be worthy of the gospel of Christ.

5. **ASSIGNMENT**
Students to further study their citizenship here on earth.

LESSON 17
CHRISTIANITY AND GOVERNANCE

PRAYER POINT – Father, let it be well with the government of my country, in Jesus name.

PREVIOUS KNOWLEDGE – The Assistant Teacher should review the previous week's lesson after the opening prayer (by students).

TODAY'S LESSON

1. OPENING

i. ***LESSON TEXT*** – Romans 13:1-6

ii. ***MEMORY VERSE*** – "And hast made us unto our God kings and priests: and we shall reign on the earth." Revelation 5:10

iii. ***LESSON INTRODUCTION*** – Governance is an act of administration: leading and exercising authority over a group of people. God has called us into a life of influence, control and dominion. Gen. 1:28. Christians are to take charge and the issue of governance is no exception. As the light of the world, we are to dispel the darkness of unrighteousness, sycophancy, etc. Matt 5:15 -16.

TEACHER'S DIARY

i. ***LESSON AIM*** – To study about Christianity and governance.

ii. ***TEACHING OBJECTIVES*** – Through the lesson, students should be able to understand the views of God on governance and why Christians should be involved in governance. Discover some Biblical examples of those who were involved in governance. Teacher should teach/explain the three lesson outlines, summarize, conclude and evaluate lesson. Teacher should give assignment to the students from the workbook.

iii. **TEXT REVIEW**: Romans 13:1-6

Romans 13:1-6 transfers the following responsibilities to the governed.

- Subject/ submission to authority (respect). Romans 13:1
- Obedience to power (afraid of power). Romans 13:2-3
- Payment of tax (payment of tribute). Romans 13:6-7,
- Do that which is good (law abiding). Romans 13:3

The same scripture confers the following responsibilities to those in government.

- Judge/punish evil work (justice). Romans 13:3,4
- Reward good work (reward/award). Romans 13:3
- Ordained to do only what is good to the citizenry (Rule of law/fairness). Roman.13:4
- Attending continually to needs (welfare). Romans 13:6

Let the government and the governed be guided.

iv. **TEACHING METHOD** – Teacher should use the lecture teaching method.

v. **TIME MANAGEMENT** – Teacher should use the standard time for three lesson outlines.

2. LESSON OUTLINES

i. **LESSON OUTLINE A** – THE VIEW OF GOD ON GOVERNANCE

- God is the ultimate power who delegates functions to human beings, Romans 13:1; Genesis 45:8; Genesis 1:26.
- Governance/Government/ruling is a calling of the Holy Spirit. I Cor. 12:28, Rom. 12:8

CHRISTIANITY AND GOVERNANCE

- Governance /ruling is a machinery for orderliness and sanity. Titus 1:5; Judges 21:25
- God instituted governance for administration of justice and general welfare of citizenry. Psalm 72:4
- God commanded the governed to submit to those in authority (the government). Romans 13:1-2; Eph. 6:5-8
- God instituted governance as a means of serving the governed. i.e to govern is to serve. Matt. 20:25-28.

CLASS ACTIVITY – What are those services which government should provide for its citizenry to make it relevant to the people.

ii. ***LESSON OUTLINES B*** – WHY CHRISTIANS SHOULD BE INVOLVED IN GOVERNANCE.
- To provide/ effect positive and lasting change. Gen. 1:26; 41:33-38.
- To make righteous laws and decrees which will promote national progress. Proverb 14:34
- To bring blessing and breakthrough to the citizens. Prv.11:11
- To avoid paying costly price for bad leadership. Romans 13:12
- It is God's will and instruction. I Peters 2 :13-15

iii. ***LESSON OUTLINE C*** – BIBLICAL EXAMPLES OF THOSE WHO GOVERNED
- Noah and the civil governance. Gen. 9:1-3
- Joseph and the Egyptians Government. Gen. 41:40-41
- Joshua and the administrative style of governance. Joshua 1:1-3; Judges 2:7
- Deborah triumphant administration in the days of intimidation and adversity. Judges 4:4; 15-16.
- Nehemiah liberal administration for reconstruction and prosperity. Nehemiah 5:14-15.
- Daniel's position as "Chief of Governor" and the First President (Parliamentary and Presidential) provided administration of direction and excellence to Babylon. Dan.2:48

3. **SUMMARY**
   God wants His children involved in governance to fulfill His mandate and for the best interest of the governed. The Bible contains examples of God children who governed and left indelible foot prints in the path of history. Citizenry too have their duties to provide for good governance. Therefore, governance involved the government and the governed.

4. **CONCLUSION**
   God instituted Governance; it is not a secular concept or people's creation. Believers should therefore take their rightful place in deciding the destiny of their nations and turn the kingdom of this world to the kingdom of God which is God's divine mandate for us.

5. **ASSIGNMENT**
   Students to study what Christians should do to encourage good performance of government.

LESSON 18
VOTING

PRAYER POINT – Ask that the Almighty God grant all students divine wisdom and insight into the Word of God today. Pray that the wisdom of God revealed today will be translated into action.

PREVIOUS KNOWLEDGE – Teacher to review the previous week's lesson.

TODAY'S LESSON

1. OPENING

i. ***LESSON TEXT*** – Romans 13:1-7

ii. ***MEMORY VERSE*** – "Learn to do good; seek justice, rebukes the oppressor; defend the fatherless, plead for the widow." Isaiah 1:17

iii. ***LESSON INTRODUCTION*** – Politics is not dirty business! Christians are in the world though not of the world. Christians as good citizens should play their part to ensure good government. One way to do this is to vote. By voting, we exert an influence in society and have a voice in determining what laws shall control the nation. Yes, your vote as a Christian matter. Voting is a way of telling our neighbors, believers and nonbelievers alike, that we too are committed to a vision of 'thy kingdom come, thy will be done on earth.'

TEACHER'S DIARY

i. ***LESSON AIM*** – To challenge students to rise up to their civic responsibility to vote as responsible citizens and contribute meaningfully to the society and nation that they belong to.

ii. ***TEACHING OBJECTIVES AND LESSON PLAN*** – At the end of the lesson, students should be able to mention at least four reasons why they should vote as Christians. They should be able to enumerate three responsibilities of Christian voters. The objective is that they should be enlightened about the need to be responsible voters in society. This should lead to a change in attitude and commitment to the society that they belong to.

iii. ***TEXT REVIEW*** – Romans 13:1-7

We can learn from the text of today how Christian citizens of a nation should react in matters of democracy and government:

- Christians live on earth under a civilian government, vs. 1
- God commands that all Christians be subject to governing authorities, vs. 1
- Governing authorities are by God's sovereign permission, He appointed them, vs. 1
- Resisting governing authorities is resisting God's ordinance, vs. 2
- The above may result in God's judgment, vs. 2
- If you obey governing authorities, you have nothing to fear, vs. 3
- Live as a responsible citizen, vs. 5-7

iv. ***TEACHING METHOD*** – Use participatory teaching method.

v. ***TIME MANAGEMENT*** – Teacher should share teaching time equally between the two lesson outlines.

2. LESSON OUTLINES

i. ***LESSON OUTLINE A*** – WHY A CHRISTIAN SHOULD VOTE
- Voting publicly identifies that you are submitted to the authority of the political system in our nation as established by God. Rom. 13:1
- It is one way to obey God's command to seek the good of those around us and our nation as a whole, Mic. 6:8; Jam. 4:17

- To make a difference and influence the society for good, Matt. 5:13; Matt. 5:14-16
- It is a privilege not to be taken for granted, Matt. 7:6; Pr. 22:13. Not voting is a form of voting, as it will influence the outcome. Pr. 13:4. Christians need to take responsibility for their actions, as well as a lack of action, Pr. 12:24, Pr. 24:30-34
- Voting is part of our stewardship to use all the resources you have been given in ways that honor God; to waste a vote is to squander a gift, Lk. 19:12-13, 15. When Christians do not 'occupy' the devil and his cohorts are free to occupy.
- Holding political office is in the Scriptures, Gen. 45:9; Dan. 6:1-2

ii. *LESSON OUTLINE B* – RESPONSIBILITIES OF A CHRISTIAN VOTER
- Register to vote and encourage others to do so, Lk. 2:1-5. Citizens are required to be of a mature age on the electoral roll. Joseph traveled with his family as directed by the government to participate in a census.
- Be educated and familiar with what candidates up for election stand for. Policies and proposals that violate the Bible's commands for life, family, marriage, or faith should be rejected, Pr. 14:34; Pr. 11:11. Ungodly leaders can hinder our freedom. Ps. 137:1-3
- Pray for and about candidates up for nomination and seeking God's direction for His choice, 1 Sam. 16:5-13; 1 Tim. 2:1-2
- Shun idolatry of candidates and let honesty prevail, Acts 12:20-23; Matt. 27:20-24.

3. **SUMMARY**

Christians must vote as a right and privilege of citizenship. A continued failure to exercise this right is an approval for unrighteousness and moral decay to reign in any society. We must express our obedience to God by exercising our rights and privileges as citizens through voting.

4. **CONCLUSION**

   Have you contributed positively to your society by participating in voting? Are godly elected officials in government over you as a result of your participation according to Gal 6:7?

5. **ASSIGNMENT**

   Students to discuss this interesting aspect of the study of God.

LESSON 19
DIVINE CALLING

PRAYER POINT – Father, help me to respond to your calling, in Jesus name.

PREVIOUS KNOWLEDGE – Teacher should allow students to review the previous week's lesson and ensure that the students' workbooks are marked.

TODAY'S LESSON

1. OPENING

i. ***LESSON TEXT*** – Mark 3:13-15

ii. ***MEMORY VERSE*** – "Faithful is he that calleth you, who also will do it". I Thessalonians 5:24

iii. ***LESSON INTRODUCTION*** – Divine', according to Webster Dictionary, is 'pertaining to; proceeding from, or of the nature of God. A call is an invitation to something higher than an individual. Therefore, divine calling simply means a call proceeding from God. God is the Caller and whoever receives the call is the called. One of the greatest things that can happen to an individual is to be called by God. It can be a call unto salvation; this is universal in scope John 3:16; Titus 2:11 God can also call people to His service. John 15:16; Mark 3:13-15.

TEACHER'S DIARY

i. ***LESSON AIM***: To study on the examples and benefits of divine calling.

ii. ***TEACHING OBJECTIVES AND LESSON PLAN*** – After the lesson, students should be able to understand and discover some examples of divine calling benefits of obeying divine calling.

iii. ***TEXT REVIEW*** – Mark 3:13-15

The Bible passage for today's lesson specified four reasons why Jesus called and ordained the twelve disciples:

- That they should be with Him. Mark 3:14a
- To send them forth to preach. Mark 3:14b
- To have power over sicknesses. Mark 13:15a
- To cast out devils. Mark 3:15b.

Teachers who are desirous of church ordination should note the following:

- None of the twelve which Jesus ordained LOBBIED for the ordination. "He called whom he would." Mark 3:13a
- None of the twelve rejected the call. "And they came unto him". They were not forced or induced. They came willingly. Mark 3:13b
- They were not ordained for funfair. They were Ministers with portfolio. Mark 3:14-15.

Therefore, teachers and ministers of God who seek for position in the church should be well guided.

iv. ***TEACHING METHOD*** – Teacher should use participatory discussion teaching method.

v. ***TIME MANAGEMENT*** – Teacher should share the teaching time equally between the two lesson outlines.

2. LESSON OUTLINES

i. ***LESSON OUTLINE A*** – BIBLICAL EXAMPLES OF THE CALLED

Teacher should give some examples of the called (by God) and their responsibilities as stated below:

- Moses – Called to deliver the Israelites from slavery. Ex. 3, 7, 10
- Abraham - God called Abraham to become and showcase absolute trust and faith in God and His words. Genesis. 12:1-5.

- ○ The Twelve Disciples- Jesus called them to be with Him and follow Him. Luke 6:13
- ○ Apostle Paul- To preach to the Gentiles. Acts. 9:15; Acts 13:2; Acts 22:21.
- ○ Prophet Elijah- To declare the supremacy of God and His word to the Prophets of Ball, his worshipers and infidels.

CLASS ACTIVITY – Identify those things that will prove that a person is truly called by God.

ii. LESSON OUTLINE 2 – THE BENEFITS OF OBEYING DIVINE CALL
- ○ Cordial relationship with God. Exodus 3:12
- ○ Assurance of God's presence at all times. Joshua 1:5
- ○ God will send helpers of destiny to the fellow. 2 Samuel 23:14-16; 2 Tim.4:11.
- ○ God will empower the called to perform wonders such as:
  - ◊ Healing the sick
  - ◊ Setting the captive free.
  - ◊ Raising the dead.
  - ◊ Delivering the oppressed, etc. Mark 16:15-18; Act 10:38.

The faithful called will be blessed on earth and be rewarded in heaven. Matthew 19:27-29; Rev. 2:10

3. SUMMARY

God has called so many people for various assignments in the past (both in the Bible and the world). HE is still calling people today for various instructions starting from repentance to specific tasks. Hebrew 3:15-16, 4:7, Has blessed and will bless people who are faithful to their callings.

4. CONCLUSION

God's call is for everyone who is willing to come to Him. If you yield yourself to His call, He will not only use you, but will also demonstrate His power through you and make you a star in the process. To what extent do you rely on God, your Caller?

5. ASSIGNMENT
Students should identify dangers of going into ministry or starting a church without a call from God.

LESSON 20
EVERYONE HAS A SUBSTITUTE

PRAYER POINT – Father, please do not forsake and replace me, in Jesus name.

PREVIOUS KNOWLEDGE – The Assistant Teacher should review the lesson for the last week Sunday school.

TODAY'S LESSON

1. **OPENING**

    i. ***LESSON TEXT*** – 1Samuel 16:1

    ii. ***MEMORY VERSE*** – "And as Peter was coming in, Cornelius met him, and fell down at His feet, and worshiped him. But Peter took him up, saying, stand up; I myself also am a man" Acts 10:25-26.

    ii. ***LESSON INTRODUCTION*** – For someone to be indispensable means, without that person, nothing can be done. In real life, human beings try to avoid a situation whereby one man becomes all important. Only God is indispensable. Jn. 15:5b. Positions or status without Jesus is simply nothing in the sight of God. This must be a humbling revelation. Dan. 4:27-33.

TEACHER'S DIARY

    i. ***LESSON AIM*** – To study the fact that no one is indispensable except God.

    ii. ***TEACHING OBJECTIVES AND LESSON PLAN*** – After the lesson, students should be able to exercise caution in taking the place of God and understand the fact that God can replace anyone. Teacher should teach the two lesson outlines with relevant Bible references, summaries, conclude and evaluate the lesson.

iii. **TEXT REVIEW** – I Samuel 16:1

   A. God always has alternatives.
   - ◊ He replaced Saul with David. I Samuel 16:1
   - ◊ He replaced Vashti with Esther. Esther 2:4,17 2:4,17.
   - ◊ He replaced Judas with Matthias. Acts 1:26.

   B. God does not forsake His people except under some conditions stated below:
   - ◊ Disobedience like the case of Saul. I Samuel 15:26.
   - ◊ Pride like the case of Vashti. Esther 1:12
   - ◊ Covetousness/iniquity and betrayal like the case of Judas. Act 1:18

   C. God out of His abundant mercy may decide to give a second chance to anyone He removed when such person repents his ways and returns the glory due to God to Him. Dan. 4:34-37

iv. **TEACHING METHOD** – Teacher should use the lecture teaching method.

v. **TIME MANAGEMENT** – Teacher should share the teaching time equally between the two lesson outlines.

2. LESSON OUTLINES

i. **LESSON OUTLINE A** – ARE YOU TAKING THE PLACE OF GOD?
   - ❍ Because of Position and Commitment, people may be tempted to believe that they are indispensable.
   - ❍ Goliath being a champion of the Philistine army thought he was indispensable or unbeatable. But he was soon proven to be wrong. I Sam. 17:4-10.

- Nebuchadnezzar because of his great political power and authority thought there was none like him. But he soon discovered that he was wrong. Dan. 4:30-33.
- Herod after his pompous statement was consumed by maggots. He was replaced. Acts. 12:21-23.
- Pharaoh with his stubbornness and hardened heart ended in the red sea. He was replaced. Ex. 5:2.
- Believers must never take to themselves the glory that belongs to God. Isaiah 48:11b.
- Peter refused to be tempted to adduce to himself the glory that was due to God. Acts 10:25-26.
- Believers must never think of themselves to be too important than others. Matt. 20:20-21; Acts 10:25-26.

CLASS ACTIVITY – What human attitudes or gestures, etc can be interpreted to mean taking the place of God?

  ii. *LESSON OUTLINE B* – BEWARE! YOU CAN BE REPLACED.
  - No one is too big to be replaced by God. Act. 1:15 -20
  - The moment a believer turned his back to God by committing sin. He/she will be replaced by God. Roman 1:28-32; I Sam. 16:1; Genesis 4:7
  - Believers should not allow their relevance to things of God enter into their head and consequently be deceived. Mark. 8:15; Luke 12:15.
  - Believers should take heed and be guided.

3. **SUMMARY**
Do not do what looks like taking the place of God, those who do such things will be replaced by God. To avoid being replaced, believers must take heed to their attitude, conducts, thoughts, behaviors, etc.

4. **CONCLUSION**
Returning the Glory to God for all successes and achievements is a sure way to remaining relevant in God's plan. 1Cor. 4:7; 10:31.

5. **ASSIGNMENT**
   Students should study the possible consequences of being replaced by God.

LESSON 21
TOUGH JOB

PRAYER POINT – Pray for divine help and grace for students to endure trials and hardships in their place of employment.

PREVIOUS KNOWLEDGE – Teacher to review the previous week's lesson.

TODAY'S LESSON

1. OPENING

i. ***LESSON TEXT*** – Ephesians 6:5-8

ii. ***MEMORY VERSE*** – "That you also aspire to lead a quiet life, to mind your own business, and to work with your own hands, as we commanded you." 1 Thessalonian 4:11

iii. ***LESSON INTRODUCTION*** – Christians sometimes complain and murmur about their secular jobs, bosses, co-workers etc. But oftentimes, the complaints are unnecessary and challenges at work can be overcome if we allow the glory of God to shine through us. Secular (non-Christian) bosses also have a lot of complains and unsavory comments, reports and evaluations of Christians at work. Are you a delightful Christian employee or are you bringing disrepute to the kingdom with your attitude at work? Is your work environment difficult? How are you letting the light of God shine through you? We pray that the Almighty God will give you victory in your place of employment in Jesus name. Amen.

TEACHER'S DIARY

i. ***LESSON AIM*** – To challenge students to review their personal work ethics and trust in God on the subject of secular employment. Christians are challenged to make a difference in the secular workplace and not be easily defeated by challenges they may face.

ii. ***TEACHING OBJECTIVES AND LESSON PLAN*** – At the end of the lesson, students should be able to mention at least four common challenges faced by Christian employees at their work places. They should be able to enumerate at least four reasons why God allows challenges in the work place of His children. They should be able to mention some ways God give His children victory. The teacher should be encouraged to rise up in faith and translate challenges at work into opportunities to glorify God. Students should briefly discuss practical experiences and how they were able to find a godly solution to their challenges.

iii. ***TEXT REVIEW*** – Ephesians 6:5-8

The truth nuggets in this text are as follows:
- A servant is one who renders service to another, vs. 5
- Obedience to master is none negotiable, vs. 5
- Obedience must be according to flesh (means according to the dictates of the job), vs. 5
- Obedience must be with trembling and from the heart as unto God, vs. 5
- Serve with diligence and sincerity, vs. 6
- Your purpose is to honor God and glorify Him, vs. 5
- Do your job with a pure heart and without hypocrisy, vs. 6
- Your Christian character must shine through in your secular job, vs. 7
- Jesus Christ is the Master you serve, vs. 7
- God will reward your services and obedience, vs. 8

iv. ***TEACHING METHOD*** – Use the participatory teaching method.

v. ***TIME MANAGEMENT*** – Teacher should share the teaching time equally between the three lesson outlines.

2. LESSON OUTLINES

i. *LESSON OUTLINE A* – CHALLENGES AT WORK
- There will always be challenges at work and it is to be expected, Jn. 16:33; Jn. 14:27; 1 Jn. 4:4; Mt. 16:24
- Unfair and difficult workload, Ex. 1:13-14; Ex. 5:6-9
- Low or no pay, unfair remuneration changes, Lk. 15:15-16, Gen. 31:6-7, 41, Jer. 22:13
- Wicked interference, Mt. 13:24-25. It is possible for others to try to wreck your good work.
- Falsehood, Mt. 5:10-12
- Isolation because of an unwillingness to join in unrighteous acts like office visits to nightclubs, bars, ungodly advances, office politics, etc. 2 Tim. 3:12; 2 Cor. 6:14.

ii. *LESSON OUTLINE B* – PURPOSE OF CHALLENGES
- You are in your present position for a purpose, Gen. 45:5, 7. Joseph endured as a slave and prisoner for a divine purpose.
- Learn from it, pass the tests (challenges) and move on to the next level, Phil. 3:12-15
- Challenges at work build character, 2 Pet. 1:5-10
- Worker harder if this is required, Pr. 6:6-11; Pr. 10:4.
- An opportunity to improve yourself, skills, etc. Don't grumble about being passed over for promotion if you have made no attempt to improve yourself. Do you have a winning attitude with your job or are you operating as a defeated person? Gen 39:20-23.
- Introduce new initiatives at work. Pr. 19:15, 24, Pr. 20:4. Bring new skills and talents to the table.

iii. LESSON OUTLINE C – GOD WILL GIVE YOU VICTORY
- Your challenges have an expiration date, Eccl. 3:1,7; Eccl. 8:6
- God will help you, seek Him in the place of prayer, Is. 41:10; Ps. 50:15

- ○ God will reward your diligent service, 2 Cor. 4:17-18; Rom. 8:18; Matt. 25:23; Ps. 75:6-7
- ○ God will make it worthwhile for you, Rom. 8:28
- ○ Continue to shine brightly and bring godly change as instructed in Matt. 5:13-16.
- ○ We are soldiers of Christ and places of work can also a place of warfare, 2 Tim. 2:3-4.

3. SUMMARY
Brethren, are you facing challenges at work? Is yours a tough job? Are you coping well or is it difficult to continue dealing with the challenges? God is Omniscient and knows what you are enduring, but have you cried out to Him for divine intervention? Have you asked for godly counsel from other believers? Is your life endangered by the challenges at work? What options are available to you as a godly way of escape? Remember that every challenge has an expiration date.

4. CONCLUSION
Challenges at work should be expected and committed into the hands of God for a godly solution. Challenges help us to mature as Christians.

5. ASSIGNMENT
Students should discuss past problems and challenges at work and how they dealt with them in the light of this teaching.

LESSON 22
DANGER OF DRIFTING

PRAYER POINT – Pray for divine help and grace for students to stand until the Day of Rapture if the Lord tarries. Pray that the wisdom of God revealed today will be translated into positive action.

PREVIOUS KNOWLEDGE – Teacher to review the previous week's lesson.

TODAY'S LESSON

1. OPENING

i. ***LESSON TEXT*** – Hebrews 2:1-4

ii. ***MEMORY VERSE*** – "Uphold my steps in your paths that my footsteps may not slip." Psalm 17:5

iii. ***LESSON INTRODUCTION*** – The danger of drifting is not limited to the physical realm. Sometimes we are distracted when driving (cell phones, eating, etc.) and can drift into another lane thereby endangering ourselves. Sadly, it is not uncommon for Christians to drift toward destruction. Brethren, are you drifting? Would you know it if you are drifting away? Have you noticed other brethren drifting away from the faith? May the Almighty God open our eyes to see the danger of drifting away from Him today and give the grace to return to Him fully in Jesus name. Amen.

TEACHER'S DIARY

i. ***LESSON AIM*** – To challenge students to refocus and evaluate their walk with God. Many who have fallen by the wayside did not arrive there suddenly. They drifted away slowly and unconsciously.

ii. ***TEACHING OBJECTIVES AND LESSON PLAN*** – At the end of the lesson, students should be able to mention at least three points about drifting. They should be able to itemize signs to identify drifting. They should be able to mention at least four remedies of drifting. Students should be encouraged to critically evaluate their individual standing in the Lord based on the points treated. It is important that each individual be satisfied that he/she is still in faith. Students can also discuss practical ways to assist others who have obviously drifted away unknowingly. They should lay out points to help those who have drifted and restore them back to faith.

iii. ***TEXT REVIEW*** – Hebrews 2:1-4

The truth nuggets in this text are as follows:

- God has spoken – this is evident from the rest of the verse encouraging us to 'take heed,' vs. 1. Heed, according to Webster's 1913 Unabridged English Dictionary is to mind, to regard with care, to take notice of, to attend to and to observe. Another one is to take careful consideration.
- The things we have heard require more heed than ordinary. So earnest heed is required.
- It is important to listen to the doctrine of Christ with care, candor, and deep concern, vs. 1
- If we have been listening to God's commands, that is commendable, but there is need for 'more earnest heed,' that is, greater attention, care and focus, vs.1
- We have evidence of angels speaking and judgment followed disobedience, vs. 2
- Why would anyone then disregard what was spoken by the Lord Jesus Christ Himself while here on earth, vs. 3
- The commands of our Lord Jesus Christ was also conveyed to us by His disciples and a great cloud of witnesses, vs. 3
- God also honored His Word through His disciples with great signs and wonders following, vs. 4

iv. ***TEACHING METHOD*** – Use the participatory teaching method.

v. ***TIME MANAGEMENT*** – Teacher should share the teaching time equally between the three lesson outlines.

2. LESSON OUTLINES

i. ***LESSON OUTLINE A*** – DRIFTING
- Drifting is effortless, all you have to do is to stop rowing against the wind and the boat will start to drift. Heb. 2:1
- It is an unconscious process because in a boat the undercurrent is not visible on the surface. A church can drift into error and an individual Christian can wander away from the core truths in the Scriptures. 1 Tim. 4:1; Pet. 2:3; Deut. 4:9
- Drifting is never upstream or against the tide because faithfulness to the Lord is like rowing upstream. 2 Pet. 1:5; 2 Pet. 3:18. Once you stop growing, adding to your faith, the slide downstream or backwards starts.
- Drifting is a hazard to the drifter and to others. Eph. 4:14; Heb. 13:9
- A shipwreck is possible if one is adrift without check. Lk. 21:34

ii. ***LESSON OUTLINE B*** – SIGNS OF DRIFTING
- Dwindling thirst for the Word and prayer, 1Thess.5:17; 1 Pet. 4:7; Col. 4:2; Lk. 18:1
- Diminishing desire to be with God's people, Ps 122:1; 2 Tim. 4:10; 4:9-12; 1 Cor. 15:33. Rather enjoying popularity with worldly friends as an 'easy going or liberal Christian'.
- Reluctance to share the gospel, 1 John 2:15; Rm. 1:16; Mk. 8:38; Ps. 40:9-10. When a Christian no longer has the desire to take the message of salvation to others, he is drifting!
- Love for the things of the world, 1 Jn. 2:15-17; 2 Tim. 3:4; Matt. 6:24; Jam. 4:4.

iii. ***LESSON OUTLINE C*** – REMEDIES AGAINST DRIFTING

- Keep rowing and spiritually speaking, this involves diligence, 2 Pet. 1:5-10. You must press on as there is no place for early retirement, Phil. 3:12-15
- Watch out for temptation (undercurrents), Gal. 5:16-18; Rm. 6:12. Never underestimate the desire of the devil to distract you.
- Make sure your anchor is strong and sure, Col. 2:6-7; Eph. 4:14-15; Eph. 3:16-18; Mt. 7:13-14

3. SUMMARY

Brethren, are you drifting? The danger is real and must not be treated with levity. It would be foolish to do so. Many have drifted away from the Lord, and arrogance can make one say, it cannot happen to me. Have you noticed any signs of drifting in your life? Has your prayer life diminished? Do you spend quality time in the Word to receive instructions and fellowship with God? Are you unduly attracted to keeping up with worldly fashions, language, manners? Have you lost the desire to save those who are lost? When did you win a soul last?

4. CONCLUSION

Your salvation was bought at a price and a dear one too, the precious Blood of Jesus Christ. Make every effort to re-trace your step if you have wandered away from the faith.

1. ASSIGNMENT

Students to look inwards and discuss practical ways of restoration for those who have obviously drifted away.

LESSON 23
DEPRESSION IN THE LIFE OF A BELIEVER – Part 1

PRAYER POINT – Pray against the spirit of depression and suicide in your life and family.

PREVIOUS KNOWLEDGE – Class teacher should review the previous week lessons with the students.

TODAY'S LESSON

1. OPENING

i. ***LESSON TEXT*** – 1 Samuel 30:1-14

ii. ***MEMORY VERSE*** – "Why are you cast down, O my soul? And why are you disquieted within me? Hope in God, for I shall yet praise Him for the help of His countenance," Psalm 42:5

iii. ***LESSON INTRODUCTION*** – Depression is a common condition affecting millions of people worldwide. Some Christians are not immune. Today more and more people are suffering from the direct and indirect effects of depression and its consequences.

TEACHER'S DIARY

i. ***LESSON AIM*** – To ensure that students know about depression and the likely causes.

ii. ***TEACHING OBJECTIVES AND LESSON PLAN*** – At the end of the lesson, students should be able to define what constitute depression and understand the various causes of depression. To achieve these objectives, teacher should explain both outlines as stated in the

DEPRESSION IN THE LIFE OF A BELIEVER – PART 1

teacher's manual allow students to participate in the class activities, summarize and conclude the lesson.

iii. **TEXT REVIEW** – 1 Samuel 30:1-14

iv. **TEACHING METHOD** – Teacher should use discussion method.

v. **TIME MANAGEMENT** – Teacher should spend more teaching on lesson 2 outlines.

2. LESSON OUTLINES

i. **LESSON OUTLINE A** – DEPRESSION DEFINED

- Depression is defined differently depending on who you ask. Some associate depression with the feelings of sadness, sorrow, despondency or feelings of rejection and gloom.
- This outline limits depression to what physicians describe as clinical depression with a little variation (for example a diagnosis of clinical depression can only be made after six months of the above mentioned symptoms).
- Regardless of the definition, we all know when we are not ourselves. A depressed mood affects how you feel, think and behave.
- Consider the situation with the children of Israel at the Wilderness of Sin, Ex. 16:1-3.
- Consider the situation of Job in Job 3:11.
- Depression could impact your relationships, your health and relationships; the men of David thought of stoning him at Ziglag, 1 Sam. 30:1-6.
- It can be expressed as emotional symptoms or physical symptoms and if not identified and quickly resolved the consequences can be enormous it can lead to diminished happiness, poor productivity, increased loss, physical illness and premature death.
- It can also cause decline in cognitive function, increased risk taking and poor judgment

ii. *LESSON OUTLINE B* – CAUSES OF DEPRESSION

Causes of depression could include the following:

- Inherited trait- Anyone with a strong family history of Major depression with or without suicide is at increased risk from suffering from depression.
- Biochemical changes- some people suffer from depression after traumatic brain injuries that affect the production and proper balance of certain brain hormones. Others suffer the same as a results of side effects of medications (some malaria medicines affects brain hormones to the effects that it produces depression until the medicine is stopped)
- Situational- Major negative life events can lead to a depressed mood, examples include the death of a loved one, major illness (2 Kings 20:1-3) divorce, relationship changes, new environment (Psalm 137:10), legal issues, lawsuits, false criminal charges etc etc), financial loss, job losses, harmful threats (Esther 4:13)
- Spiritual attacks-1 Samuel 16:14-16-(evil Spirit on Saul; Isaiah 61:3 (Spirit of heaviness) Not every depression is caused by Devilish Spiritual attacks but the bible describes a Spirit of heaviness. Discernment is needed to identify this kind especially when no obvious cause of depression is identified. This kind does not usually respond to medical intervention but by prayers freedom and joy can be obtained.
- Substance abuse and addictions- The use of mind altering drugs can sometimes lead to depression.
- Depression may also develop as a result of addictions, for example addiction to pornography or gluttony that may lead to eating disorders etc etc.
- Stress- Untamed and prolonged stressful situations in addition to those mentioned in C above can lead to depression. Examples include frustrations from persistent negative criticisms, inadequate sleep, negative outcomes, failure to meet expectations and excessive burden bearing.
- Please share any insight or comments on the definition, causes and life experiences on depression. God bless you.

3. **SUMMARY**

    It is possible for a Christian to be depressed, but not all cases of depression are spiritual attack.

4. **CONCLUSION:**

    There are several reasons for this knowledge. Can you recall situations of depression due to the causes above? Pray today that the Lord will intervene in the situations of people you perceive to be depressed.

LESSON 24
OVERCOMING DEPRESSION IN THE LIFE OF A BELIEVER – Part 2

PRAYER POINT – Pray against the spirit of depression and suicide in your life and family.

PREVIOUS KNOWLEDGE – Class teacher should review the previous week lessons with the students.

TODAY'S LESSON

1. **OPENING**

    i. *LESSON TEXT* – 1 Kings 19:1-14

    ii. *MEMORY VERSE* – "............. and came and sat down under a broom tree. And he prayed that he might die, and said, "It is enough! Now, LORD, take my life, for I am no better than my father's!" 1 Kings 19:4

    iii. *LESSON INTRODUCTION* – Part one of this lesson treated the definition and causes of depression. In this lesson, we intend to look at signs of depressed. We equally would study the stages of depression and available help to a depressed believer. It is our prayer the Holy Spirit will teach us today in the name of Jesus Christ.

TEACHER'S DIARY

    i. *LESSON AIM* – To ensure that students know about depression and the likely causes.

    ii. *TEACHING OBJECTIVES AND LESSON PLAN*

At the end of the lesson, students should be able to define what constitutes depression and know the available helps. Everyone should examine themselves and look for signs and traits of depression. Get help as soon as possible.

iii. **TEXT REVIEW** – 1 Kings 19:1-14
- Jezebels threated Elijah vs 1-3.
- When Ahab told Jezebel about Elijah killing all of her prophets, she's was shocked and unhappy.
- Instead of Jezebel repenting she made a vow to kill within 24 hours the man who exposed the lies of Baal worship. "Let the gods kill me if I fail to do to you what you did to my prophets by this time tomorrow."
- Elijah was greatly discouraged and overwhelmed with fear because all that happened on Mount Carmel did not bring total repentance and mourning to Israel. So Elijah ran to hide in the wilderness.
- Elijah became depressed and suicidal. Vs 4.
- He sat down under a tree and tells the Lord "Now, Lord, take my life, for I am no better than my father's"
- He apparent felt he had failed in ministry because he was a sinner as the rest of his ancestors.
- God ministered to him physically and spiritually. Vs 5-8.
- He was tired and exhausted. God's mercy rested and refreshed him with good sleep.
- His angels nourished/replenished him with delicious food/drink.
- Twice the Lord ministered to him with sleep/ food/drink, so that his heart, brain and muscles would recover well for the next assignment.

"Arise and eat, because the journey is too great for you." So he arose, and ate and drank; and he went in the strength of that food forty days and forty nights as far as Horeb, the mountain of God"

- Instead of rebuke or remonstrance, chiding or chastisement; God lovingly and mercifully restored him spiritually as he walked with him for 40 days and 40 nights.

- God allowed Elijah to vent/express his frustrations. Vs 9-10
- God asked Elijah a question so that he could speak to the Lord freely and to unburden his heart.
- Elijah protested "I have faithfully served You. Now look at the danger I am in." To Elijah - and many servants of God, it seemed unfair that a faithful servant of God should be made to suffer.
- "I alone am left" This was not accurate, but this was how Elijah felt. (1 Kings 18:22).

Discouraging times make God's servants feel more isolated and alone than they are.

- God reveals Himself to Elijah. Vs 9-10
- God knew what the depressed and discouraged Elijah needed. He needed a personal encounter with God "Go out, and stand on the mountain before the Lord"
- "Behold, the Lord passed by":God appeared to Elijah, not in the earth-shaking phenomenon of wind, thunder, fire and earthquakes, but in "a still small voice." 'a voice of gentle silence,' as if silence had become audible (Zachariah 4:6)
- God reassigned Elijah back to work. Vs 13-15 what are you doing here, Elijah? God asked Elijah the same question.
- The best thing God did for Elijah, was giving him more work to do for Him. He sent him off about his Master's business again.
- Elijah came terrified, distressed, depressed and suicidal; but now he goes back with the strength, boldness and power of God never to be afraid of Jezebel nor any king.

iv. ***TEACHING METHOD*** – Teacher should use discussion method.

v. ***TIME MANAGEMENT*** – Teacher should spend more teaching time on lesson 2 outlines.

CLASS ACTIVITY Teacher should divide the class

2. LESSON OUTLINES

i. ***LESSON OUTLINE A*** – DEPRESSION DEFINED

Depression is defined differently depending on who you ask. Some associate depression with the feelings of sadness, sorrow, despondency or feelings of rejection and gloom. This outline limits depression to what physicians describe as clinical depression with a little variation (for example a diagnosis of clinical depression can only be made after six months of the above mentioned symptoms). Regardless of the definition, we all know when we are not ourselves. A depressed mood affects how you feel, think and behave. Consider the situation with the children of Israel at the Wilderness of Sin, Ex. 16:1-3. Consider the situation of Job in Job 3:11. Depression could impact your relationships, your health and relationships; the men of David thought of stoning him to death at Ziglag, 1 Sam. 30:1-6. It can be expressed as emotional symptoms or physical symptoms and if not identified and quickly resolved the consequences can be enormous it can lead to diminished happiness, poor productivity, increased loss, physical illness and premature death. It can also cause decline in cognitive function, increased risk taking and poor judgment

ii. ***LESSON OUTLINE B*** – CAUSES OF DEPRESSION

Causes of depression could include the following:

Inherited trait.

- Anyone with a strong family history of Major depression with or without suicide is at increased risk from suffering from depression.

Biochemical changes.

- Some people suffer from depression after traumatic brain injuries that affects the production and proper balance of certain brain hormones. Others suffer the same as a results of side effects of medications (some malaria medicines affects brain hormones to the effects that it produces depression until the medicine is stopped)

Situational.

- Major negative life events can lead to a depressed mood, examples include the death of a loved one, major illness (2 Kings 20:1-3) divorce, relationship changes, new environment (Psalm 137:10), legal issues, lawsuits, false criminal charges etc etc), financial loss, job losses, harmful threats (Esther 4:13)

Spiritual attacks.

- 1 Samuel 16:14-16-(evil Spirit on Saul; Isaiah 61:3 (Spirit of heaviness) Not every depression is caused by Devilish Spiritual attacks but the bible describes a Spirit of heaviness. Discernment is needed to identify this kind especially when no obvious cause of depression is identified. This kind does not usually respond to medical intervention but by prayers freedom and joy can be obtained.

Substance abuse and addictions.

- The use of mind altering drugs can sometimes lead to depression while the reverse can also occur. Depression may also develop as a result of addictions, for example addiction to pornography or gluttony that may lead to eating disorders.

Stress.

- Untamed and prolonged stressful situations in addition to those mentioned in C above can lead to depression. Examples include frustrations from persistent negative criticisms, inadequate sleep, negative outcomes, failure to meet expectations and excessive burden bearing.

3. **SUMMARY**
It is possible for a Christian to be depressed, but not all cases of depression are spiritual attack.

4. **CONCLUSION**
There are several reasons for this knowledge. Can you recall situations of depression due to the causes above? Pray today that the Lord will intervene in the situations of people you perceive to be depressed.

5. **ASSIGNMENT**
Students should study causes of depression caused by spiritual attack.

LESSON 25
THE FEAR OF THE LORD

PRAYER POINT – Ask the Lord to plant His fear in the hearts of all believers.

PREVIOUS KNOWLEDGE – Teacher asks students to narrate their experiences when dealing with those sins which they had not hitherto conquered before the previous week's lesson.

The teacher should remind the class what the previous lesson was all about.

TODAY'S LESSON

1. OPENING

i. ***LESSON TEXT*** – Psalm 111

ii. ***MEMORY VERSE*** - "The fear of the LORD is the beginning of knowledge: but fools despise wisdom and instruction." Proverbs 1:7

iii. ***LESSON INTRODUCTION*** – God forbids the fear of the devil and its evil works such as diseases and arrows of death - Psalm 91:5. Why is this so? It is because the devil is not the Almighty. The devil would be bound in chains in judgment and be cast into the lake of fire alongside with the beast and the false prophet - Rev. 20:10. Instead of fearing the devil, the scriptures command us to fear God. We shall discover in our lesson of today what it means to fear the Lord and why the whole world in general and believers in particular should fear the Lord.

TEACHER'S DIARY

i. ***LESSON AIM*** - To teach what the fear of God means and the result of fearing God.

THE FEAR OF THE LORD

ii. **TEACHING OBJECTIVE** - At the end of the lesson, students should be able to explain the meaning of the fear of God, how to fear the Lord and the result of fearing God.

iii. **TEXT REVIEW** – Psalm 111

Ten reasons we should fear the Lord:
- His works are great - Ps. 111:2.
- He is an honorable and glorious God - vs. 3.
- He is a righteous God - vs. 3.
- He is a wonderful and gracious God - vs. 4.
- He supplies all our needs - vs. 5.
- He is full of power - vs. 6.
- His works are excellent - vs. 7.
- His judgments and commandments are righteous and true - vs. 8.
- He is the Redeemer, holy and revered God - vs. 9.
- His fear brings wisdom and good understanding - vs. 10.

iv. **TEACHING METHOD** – Use lecture method.

v. **TIME MANAGEMENT** – Teacher should share the teaching time equally between the two lesson outlines.

2. LESSON OUTLINES

i. **LESSON OUTLINE A** – WHAT IT MEANS TO FEAR THE LORD

   a. What it means?

   - Deep feeling that it is mandatory to obey the word of God.
   - Giving absolute reverence to the word of God.
   - Irrevocable decision to serve God always.
   - Unalloyed obedience to the commandment of God.

   b. What it could be likened to:

- ◊ Treasure to him that has it - Proverbs 15:16.
- ◊ A fountain of life that flows and waters anyone who possesses it - Pro. 14:27.
- ◊ The spiritual condition for believers' blessings - Psalm 128:1.

Please read and apply, Dan.6:13; Eccl. 12:13; Pro. 8:13.

ii. ***LESSON OUTLINE B* – WHY I MUST FEAR THE LORD**
- ○ God commanded it.
- ○ His holiness - Rev. 15:4.
- ○ His greatness - Dan. 10:12-17.
- ○ His goodness - 1 Sam.12:24.
- ○ He forgives all sins - Ps. 130:4.
- ○ His coming judgment - Rev. 14:7.

Teacher should apply the points given under the text review.

i. LESSON OUTLINE C – WHY IT IS NECESSARY TO FEAR GOD
- ○ To worship the Lord - Ps. 5:7.
- ○ To remain in service - Ps. 2:11.
- ○ To keep us from sin - Exo. 20:20.
- ○ For administration of justice - 2 Chro. 19:6-9.
- ○ For good government - 2 Sam. 23:3.
- ○ For the perfecting of holiness in our Christian lives - 2 Cor. 7:1.

ii. LESSON OUTLINE D – RESULTS OF FEARING GOD
- ○ It brings pleasure to the Lord - Ps. 147:11.
- ○ Makes our enemies to reconcile with us.
- ○ Brings pardon for sin (pities) - Ps. 103:13.
- ○ Makes a believer acceptable to God - Acts 10:35.
- ○ Brings mercy.
- ○ Brings blessings - Ps. 42:1.
- ○ Brings long life - Pro. 10:27.

- Brings answers to prayers - Ps. 145:19.
- Separates one from evil - Pro. 16:6.
- Brings confidence - Pro. 14:26.
- Destroys the fear of gods - Is. 8:12-13; 2 Kings 17:38.
- Terminates the fear of calamities - Luke 21:25-28.

3. SUMMARY
The Lord will definitely bless any person that fears Him.

4. CONCLUSION
Fear the Lord God Almighty.

5. ASSIGNMENT
Students should read at home Hebrews 11:1-16 and note the key points raised in the passage.

LESSON 26

THE SECOND QUARTER INTERACTIVE SESSION

Welcome to the Second Interactive Session!

Your privilege:

- To ask questions on treated lessons for clarity
- To give critical appraisal of the outline
- To give useful suggestions towards better performance
- To give useful spiritual contributions

LESSON 27
FAITH NOT COVETOUSNESS

PRAYER POINT – Ask the Lord to plant His fear in the heart of all believers.

PRECIOUS KNOWLEDGE – Teachers asks the students to explain what they understand by covetousness a how it relates to faith.

TODAY'S LESSON

1. OPENING

i. ***LESSON TEXT*** – 2 Kings 5:20-27

ii. ***MEMORY VERSE*** – "Let your conduct be without covetousness be content with such things as you have. For He Himself has said, "I will never leave you nor forsake you." Hebrews 13:5.

iii. ***LESSON AIM***: To study contentment in whatever you have

iv. ***TEACHING OBJECTIVE***: At the end of the lesson, students should be able to enumerate the characteristics of covetousness.

v. ***LESSON INTRODUCTION*** – Covetousness is a serious desire to possess what belongs to another person. People at times claim what belongs to another "by faith". It is the root of very many other sins, which include, lying (II Kings 5:22-25), theft (Joshua 7:21), murder (Ezekiel 22:12) and many other sins. Demand should be compared to income and not to what somebody else has.

TEACHER'S DIARY

i. ***TEXT REVIEW*** – 2 Kings 5:20-27
- Inability to control one's appetite for material things is a major cause of covetousness – vs. 20

- One should be careful with his eyes, as it is one of the gates to the body – vs. 20
- The desire for covetousness has a force that pushes people to run – vs. 21
- Covetousness comes with lying – vs. 22, 25
- One who is covetous will acquire both necessities and irrelevant things – vs. 23
- Deceit is one of the sins that covetousness brings – vs. 24
- No one can hide from God – vs. 26
- God knows even the intent of the heart; some things listed were in Ghazi's heart – vs. 26
- Covetousness has serious negative repercussions – vs. 27.

ii. **TEACHING METHOD** – Use discussion teaching method.

2. **LESSON OUTLINES**

   i. *LESSON OUTLINE A* – CHARACTERISTICS OF COVETOUSNESS
   - The object of desire could be legitimate or not. Luke. 12:13-15. It is the yardstick by which any other act is measured as to rightness or wrongness – Ezekiel 33:31
   - The desire is made legitimate by spiritualizing it – Acts 8:18-23; Romans 1:28; Titus 1:15
   - They could even take it to God in prayer – Jeremiah 17:9; Numbers 22:7-22; James 4:3-4
   - It is already a sin even before any action is taken or no action is taken because it has been conceived. II Sam. 11; 12:1-7; Matt. 5:27-28; James 1:14-15; Hosea 10:13; Matthew 7:17
   - A price value is attached to the desire. I Kings 21:2; II Peter 2:1-3; Acts 24:26; II Peter 2:15
   - Covetousness is selfish, thinking only of one's needs without any consideration of others. Esther. 5:9-13; James 4:3; Genesis 25:31; 27:6-29; I Kings 21:2-16

ii. ***LESSON OUTLINE B*** – A BIG DIFFERENCE
- Faith is God cantered whereas covetousness is self-centred, Genesis 31:7; 1 Samuel 15:9
- One is done to edify the body of Christ and invariably God whereas the other is to glorify flesh – 1 Corinthians 12:31; 14:39
- Faith increases one whereas covetousness can lead to death – Proverbs 1:19; 28:16
- There is a curse on the covetous whereas blessings follow faith – Jude 1:11
- Covetousness is worldly biased but faith of God – 1 Corinthians 10:31; Deuteronomy 10:12.

3. **SUMMARY**
God hates worldliness because the love of God is not in anyone who loves the world. Faith and covetousness don't go together. God expects that all we do to glorify Him and this is possible when one hates covetousness.

4. **CONCLUSION**
We cannot be a child of God and at the same time be covetous; we have a choice.

5. **ASSIGNMENT**
Students should read 1 Kings 21:1-16 and note the key points about covetousness raised in the text.

LESSON 28
THE MAN JESUS

PRAYER POINT – Ask the Lord to make Himself known to you the more through today's lesson.

PREVIOUS KNOWLEDGE – The teacher reminds the students the basic facts contained in the previous week's lesson.

TODAY'S LESSON

1. OPENING

i. **LESSON TEXT** – Hebrews 2:3-18

ii. **MEMORY VERSE** – Therefore, in all things He had to be made like His brethren, that He might be a merciful and faithful High Priest in things pertaining to God, to make propitiation for the sins of the people Heb. 2:17.

iii. **LESSON AIM** – To study the human nature of Christ.

iv. **TEACHING OBJECTIVE** – At the end of the lesson, students should be able to prove beyond doubt that Christ was a human being while on earth and should be able to explain the benefits of His being a human being to believers.

v. **LESSON INTRODUCTION** – One of the issues that our text for today sets to address is the human nature of Christ. Was Christ only God or a Spirit while on earth? Why did He take upon Himself the form of man? Of what benefit is His human nature to us? These are some of the issues to be discussed in today's lesson.

TEACHER'S DIARY

i. **TEXT REVIEW** – Hebrews 2:3-18

Christ was man while on earth

- Hebrews 2:7 and 9 compares "Man", you and I with Christ. It states that both were made lower than the angels.
- Both Man and Christ were crowned with glory and honor.
- Both have control over all things created by God.
- Both were sanctified - vs. 11.
- Both were for signs and wonders.
- Both were partakers of flesh and blood - vs. 14.
- He was not angel but of the seed of Abraham as other believers - vs. 16.
- He was like unto His brethren - vs. 17.
- He suffered as men suffer.
- He was tempted as men are tempted

Thank God for sending Jesus Christ in the form of Man so that He could fully understand our human feelings and to succor us in our areas of weaknesses. Teacher should apply appropriately the above points to lesson outlines 1 and 2.

ii. *LESSON CHALLENGE* – Christ was man while on earth and not God. If He overcame, you too can overcome.

iii. *TEACHING METHOD* – Use lecture teaching method.

2. LESSON OUTLINES

i. *LESSON OUTLINE A* – PROOFS THAT JESUS WAS HUMAN

  a. Proof of His human nature.
  - He had human ancestry.
  - He had a mother and brothers.
  - He was of the lineage of David.
  - He had flesh, blood and bones.
  - He had body, soul and spirit.

- He ate, walked, slept, preached, died but resurrected.

Please apply appropriately the following scriptures: Luke 2:7; Gal. 4:4; Acts 13:22-23; John 1:14; Hebrews 2:14; Matt. 26:12.

b. Every believer must believe that Christ came in the flesh.

c. Everyone who disbelieves that Christ came in the flesh belongs to the anti-Christ - 1 John 4:3.

d. The spirit of the anti-Christ disbelieves this important fact that Christ was man while He was on earth.

ii. ***LESSON OUTLINE B*** – HE OBEYED LAWS OF HUMAN DEVELOPMENT
- He was born as a baby, crawled as an infant and grew as an adult - Luke 2:40.
- He was inquisitive as other babies were - Luke 2:46.
- He grew physically and mentally - Lk. 2:52.
- He was taught obedience like all other human children - Hebrews 5:8.
- He tasted suffering like any other human being.
- He was persecuted more than any other human being - Heb. 2:10.
- He worked hard like any other human being as carpenter up till the age of thirty - Mark 6:3.
- He was tempted like any other human being.
- He died a painful death and was buried like any other human being - Heb. 9:27.

iii. LESSON OUTLINE C – BENEFITS THAT ACCRUE TO US FROM HIS HUMANITY
- He was a thirsty and hungered therefore he was able to provide for the needs of believers who are hungry and thirsty - Matt. 4:2.
- During His earthly ministry, He once became weary and tired so He is able to help the tired and weary believers and give them strength - John 4:6; Isaiah 40:30-31.

- Because He slept when He was tired even on the sea, He is able to give sleep to His beloved - Ps. 127:2; Ps. 121:4.
- He knows the extent of our endurance and therefore able to console us in sorrow and grief - John 11:33, 35.

CLASS ACTIVITY – How is Christ different from man?

3. **SUMMARY**
Because Christ was both man and God, He is able to understand our human feelings and respond to them as God.

4. **CONCLUSION**
Christ is both man and God.

5. **ASSIGNMENT**
Students should read the following scriptures at home: Mk. 10:21; John 11:35; Matt. 14:23; Heb. 4:15, 7:14; Gal. 4:4-5

LESSON 29
LIKE FATHER LIKE SON

PRAYER POINT – Father, let me be like Jesus in anointing and good work, in Jesus name.

PREVIOUS KNOWLEDGE – Teacher should allow the students to review the previous week's lesson through guided questions on Memory Verse, Lesson Outlines, Summary and Conclusion.

TODAY'S LESSON

1. **OPENING**

    i. ***LESSON TEXT*** – Mark 16:15-18

    ii. ***MEMORY VERSE*** – "How God anointed Jesus of Nazareth with the Holy Ghost and with power: who went about doing good, and healing all that were oppressed of the devil; for God was with him." Acts 10:38

    iii. ***LESSON INTRODUCTION*** – The new man in Christ (2 Cor.5:17) is easily identified by a sanctified and Holy Spirit controlled life (Rom.8:14). He must therefore, operate a powerful ministry, like father like son, and in proof producing ministry. May the watering ministry of the Holy Spirit refresh us today as we study, in Jesus Name. Amen.

TEACHER'S DIARY

   i. ***LESSON AIM*** – To study how to operate in powerful and proof producing ministry.

   ii. ***TEACHING OBJECTIVES AND LESSON PLAN*** – At the end of the lesson, students should be able to discover how to operate powerful and proof producing ministry like the Lord Jesus Christ. Teacher should allow the students to review the previous lesson.

iii. ***TEXT REVIEW*** – Mark 16:15-18
"THE COMMAND"
- Jesus said, "Go into all the world," Mark 16:15
- The command did not contain exceptional clause like "You may go, if you go or you can go" v.15
- The command has a Terms of Reference- "Preach the Gospel". The gospel is the core message of the commission. V15
- The command has specific audience- "Every creature" all human beings on earth without any discrimination. V15.
- The command has blessing for right respondents "Believe it, be baptized and be saved.V.16
- The command has punishment for defiance- "Believe not and be dammed/condemned/judged". V.16, John 3:18. 36.
- The command has mighty authority backing it.
    - It shall be accompanied with signs.
    - Devil will be cast out. V.17
    - They will speak with new tongue.
    - Serpent will not hurt them.
    - The sick will be healed/recover.
- What a command to obey!

iv. ***TEACHING METHOD*** – Teacher should use the lecture teaching method.

v. ***TIME MANAGEMENT*** – Teacher should share the teaching time equally between the two lesson outlines.

2. LESSON OUTLINES

i. ***LESSON OUTLINE A*** – 'LIKE FATHER LIKE SON' IN POWERFUL MINISTRY

- The Lord Jesus Christ is our perfect example in Ministry. Acts 2:22
- He went about preaching, , healing and delivering the oppressed. Acts 10:38
- He was outstanding and known for signs and wonders because God was with him. Mark 1:14-15, 21-22, 40-45
- God expects the believers, who are now new men, to be like the Saviour in ministry. Mark 16:15-18
- The believers carry the Holy Spirit like the Lord Jesus and should therefore preach the gospel both at home and abroad.
- The believers carry the mandate to go and preach the gospel to all nations
- The believers have the assurance of divine presence of God. Matthew 28:18-20

CLASS ACTIVITY – How can believers operate like the Lord Jesus Christ in Ministry?

ii. **LESSON OUTLINE B**: PROOF- PRODUCING MINISTRY
- The book of Acts of Apostle contains records of proof of the power of the Holy Spirit working wonders. Mark 16:20.
- The Apostles' experiences are challenges for believers to follow. Acts 2:14-37; 38-41; 42-47.
- Believers (New man) must be a vessel unto honor and loaded with the following anointing:
  ◊ Anointing to heal. Acts 3:1-9
  ◊ Anointing in power- evangelism. Act 4:7-14
  ◊ Anointing to discern and judge iniquity promptly. Act 5:1-11
  ◊ Anointing for signs and wonders. Acts 5:12; Act 6:8
  ◊ Anointing to bear fruits that will abide. John 15:16; Acts 14:1.

3. **SUMMARY**

The Bible contains proof of anointing-oriented ministry of the Lord Jesus Christ, and the apostle operated Wonder-Pack ministry of signs and wonders. Believers of today too can prayerfully emulate their examples.

4. **CONCLUSION**

   Decide today to operate in a powerful and proof-producing ministry. Get connected to the Author and Finisher of your faith, the Lord Jesus Christ.

5. **ASSIGNMENT**

   Students should study why some believers are not operating like Jesus Christ in the Ministry.

LESSON 30
UNITY IN THE CHURCH

PRAYER POINT – Pray that the spirit of unity and oneness will prevail in the church.

PREVIOUS KNOWLEDGE – Teacher asks a student to review the previous week's lesson.

TODAY'S LESSON

1. OPENING

i. ***LESSON TEXT*** – Ephesians 4:1-6

ii. ***MEMORY VERSE*** – "So we, being many, are one body in Christ, and individually members of one another." Romans 12:5

iii. ***LESSON INTRODUCTION*** – One of the biggest challenges facing the body of Christ today is the difficulty in being united. This is despite the specific instructions that Jesus Christ left His church on the need to be united. It goes without saying that the enemy is able to infiltrate the church because of the lack of fellowship and unity.

TEACHER'S DIARY

i. ***LESSON AIM*** – To draw attention to the crucial and important need for unity in the body of Christ as commanded by our Lord Jesus Christ.

ii. ***TEACHING OBJECTIVES AND LESSON PLAN*** – At the end of the lesson, students should be able to understand the need for unity and oneness in the body of Christ at large and in their local assembly. To explain this objective, the teacher brings to attention of the students, the fact that our physical bodies are made up of countless number of parts to function as one body. This is what God expects of His church.

iii. ***TEXT REVIEW*** – Ephesians 4:1-6: In the main text, it is apparent that there was a need to call the attention of true believers and followers of Christ to the need for unity.
- The Apostle Paul made a passionate appeal to the brethren here
- His appeal indicated that there was a problem of the lack of unity
- Staying united must be a deliberate act on the part of believers. Verse 3 states 'endeavoring to keep the unity of the Spirit in the bond of peace.'

iv. ***TEACHING METHOD*** – Use the lecture method

v. ***TIME MANAGEMENT*** – Teacher should share the teaching time equally between the two lesson outlines.

2. LESSON OUTLINES

i. ***LESSON OUTLINE A*** – NATURE AND PURPOSE OF UNITY
- The Scriptures is very clear to us about the need to fellowship in unity and operate in one accord. The need for unity in the body of Christ and in our local fellowship is like the need for our body parts to be united to function properly. Romans 12:3-5. 1 Corinthians 12:12-22. No part of the body is dispensable. Even the weakest part is needed and no part of the human body can live or thrive in isolation.
- Not only are we members of one body, but we are also members of one another, Ephesians 4:25, Unity in the church and body of Christ must cut across race, tribe, tongue, color, etc. Colossians 3:9-11.
- The primary purpose of unity is that we may be effective witnesses as we lead others to Christ, John 17:18-21

CLASS ACTIVITY – Students to comment on how well they think their body parts would function independent of each other.

ii. ***LESSON OUTLINE B*** – Expressions of Unity

Unity in the church and body of Christ is expressed in several ways. We cannot claim to be united if we do not manifest some of the following:

- Fellowship with God. Psalm 122:1-2, 2 Corinthians 6:14-18, Isaiah 2:1-3. Fellowship with the Father will definitely lead to fellowship with one another.
- Meeting together. Acts 2:46, 1 Corinthians 14:26, Hebrews 10:23-25. We cannot claim to be united if we do not actively seek and look forward to times of meeting together.
- Sharing resources. Acts 2:44-45, Romans 15:26, Philippians 4:14-18. True unity makes us care deeply for others with a great desire to share resources.
- Through suffering. 1 Corinthians 12:26. In a united church, when one suffers, all suffer.
- Shared spiritual blessings. Acts 2:2-3, Ecclesiastes 4:7-9, 2 Corinthians 9:12-15.
- The joy of being united is that we also share spiritual blessings.

CLASS ACTIVITY 2 – Students should consider the fact that in Noah's Ark, all the animals survived, packed together for almost a year without 'division.' Why can't we be united as Christians?

3. **SUMMARY**
   God is calling the church, the body of Christ to a higher level of unity. United we stand, divided we fall.

4. **CONCLUSION**
   The Lord is calling each individual today to 'endeavor to keep the unity of the Spirit in the bond of peace.' It is time to make a deliberate attempt to be united in fellowship.

5. **ASSIGNMENT**
   Identify ways to positively contribute to unity in your local assembly.

LESSON 31
DISUNITY IN THE CHURCH

PRAYER POINT – Pray that the spirit of unity and oneness will prevail in the church.

PREVIOUS KNOWLEDGE – Teacher asks a student to review the previous week's lesson.

TODAY'S LESSON

1. OPENING

i. ***LESSON TEXT*** – Ephesians 4:1-6

ii. ***MEMORY VERSE*** – "And if a house is divided against itself, that house cannot stand." Mark 3:25.

iii. ***LESSON INTRODUCTION*** – One of the biggest challenges facing the body of Christ today is the difficulty in being united. This is despite the specific instructions that Jesus Christ left His church on the need to be united. Disunity in the church is seriously affecting the progress that should be made in winning the world for Christ.

TEACHER'S DIARY

i. ***LESSON AIM*** – To highlight the causes of disunity in the body of Christ and bring about a change in the local assembly.

ii. TEACHING OBJECTIVE AND PLAN – At the end of the lesson, students should be able to examine themselves and identify areas where they need to change personally, for the good of their local assembly. The class should also be enlightened on areas to watch out for in general.

iii. **_TEXT REVIEW_** – Ephesians 4:1-6: In the main text, it is apparent that there was a need to call the attention of true believers and followers of Christ to the need for unity.
- The Apostle Paul made a passionate appeal to the brethren here
- His appeal indicated that there was a problem of the lack of unity
- Brethren were not operating 'with all lowliness and gentleness, with longsuffering, bearing with one another in love. It was obvious that they were disunited! 1 Corinthians 1:10

iv. **_TEACHING METHOD_** – Use discussion method

v. **_TIME MANAGEMENT_** – Teacher should share the teaching time equally between the two lesson outlines.

2. LESSON OUTLINES

i. **_LESSON OUTLINE A_** – CAUSES OF DISUNITY WITHIN HE CHURCH
- Personal ambition. Mark 9:33-34, Mark 10:35-41. When it is obvious that some members of the church are not driven by zeal but personal ambition, it causes disunity in the body.
- Ethnic tension. Acts 6:1, Hellenists were Greek-speaking Jews! Avoid tribal and race issues.
- Differences of opinion. Acts 15:37-40, Philippians 4:2. Differences of opinion can lead to division in the church. Note that the brethren prayed for Paul and Silas!
- Troublesome heretical leaders. Romans 16:17, Jude 19. Some supposed leaders in the church cause divisions subtly underground.
- Partisan spirit. 1 Corinthians 1:11-13, 1 Corinthians 3:3-4. Factions are evidence of serious division in the church.
- Greed. 1 Corinthians 11:18-21, James 4:1-2

CLASS ACTIVITY – Students to discuss other causes of disunity not listed.

ii. **_LESSON OUTLINE B_** – ACCEPTABLE DISAGREEMENT

There are some instances when it is okay to disagree in the church and body of Christ.

- ○ Heretical teachings. 2 Corinthians 11:2-6, 2 Corinthians 11:13-15, Galatians 1:6-9, 1Timothy 4:1-6, Jude 18-20. When we know the truth in the gospel, we must speak up to counter heresies, especially when there is obvious danger that souls will be led astray.
- ○ Over important gospel principles. Acts 15:1-2, 5-6, 1 Timothy 1:3-4, Galatians 2:11-16.
- ○ To call to order some who are part of the church living blatant sinful lives.

3. SUMMARY
The Bible warns against contention in the church. It's time to close ranks.

4. CONCLUSION
Disunity in the church must be avoided at all costs.

5. ASSIGNMENT
Students should identify ways of avoiding disunity and reconciliation if there is any.

LESSON 32
THE MAKING OF A CHAMPION

PRAYER POINT – Father, make me a champion from today and forever in Jesus name.

PREVIOUS KNOWLEDGE – The Teacher should review the previous week's lesson.

TODAY'S LESSON

1. OPENING

i. ***LESSON TEXT*** – Jeremiah 51:20-23

ii. ***MEMORY VERSE*** – "He raiseth up the poor out of the dust, and lifteth up the beggar from the dunghill, to set them among princes, and to make them inherit the throne of glory: for the Pillars of the Earth are the Lord's and he hath set the world upon them" 1 Samuel 2:8

iii. ***LESSON INTRODUCTION*** – A champion is the victor, the one winning, the overcomer. A champion is also the representative of the people. He is the best the people can offer. 1Samuel. 9:1-2; 17:48-51. He is excellent beyond compare. The greatest champion in history is no other person than the Lord Jesus Christ. Isaiah 9:6

TEACHER'S DIARY

i. ***LESSON AIM*** – To study on the making of a champion.

ii. ***TEACHING OBJECTIVES AND LESSON PLAN*** – After the lesson, students should be able to discover some examples of champions in the Bible and understand the truth that Jesus Christ is the greatest champion. Teacher should introduce the lesson, teach the two lesson outlines, summarize, conclude and evaluate the lesson. Teacher should give endeavor to give assignment to the students.

iii. **TEXT REVIEW** – Jeremiah 51:20-23
   - God sees believers as Battle axes and as weapons of war.
   - God intends to use the believers always for the following purpose:
     - To break nations (godless nations) into pieces. V.20
     - To destroy kingdoms (Kingdoms of darkness and demons). V.20
     - To break in pieces the horse and the riders as He did to the Pharaoh horse men in V.21, Exodus 14:23-24
     - To break in pieces the chariot and his riders. V.21, Exodus 14:25
     - To break man and woman into pieces. Men like Pharaoh, Herod, Ahab and women like Jezebel, Athaliah. II Kings 11:20, V.22
     - To break old young, young men and maid like the old and young prophets.
     - To break in pieces shepherds i.e. fake/false shepherds and their congregations. V.23
     - To break in pieces the husband men and the yoke of oxen. Isaiah 10:27.
     - To break in pieces the captain and the rulers. II Samuel 10:18
     - To render unto Babylon and Chaldea all the evil they have done in Zion like the Amalekites. V.24; I Samuel 15:2-3.

   God is preparing us for a great assignment ahead by calling us a champion- a battle axe.

iv. **TEACHING METHOD** – Teacher should use discussion teaching method.

v. **TIME MANAGEMENT** – Teacher should share the teaching time equally between the two lesson outlines.

2. LESSON OUTLINES

i. *LESSON OUTLINE* – BIBLICAL EXAMPLES OF CHAMPION

The class should discuss the champions listed below in term of their conquests victories and personalities.

- Gideon- Judges 6:15-16; 7:2-7,22
- Joshua- Joshua 1:6-7; 11-16-18
- Jephtah - Judges 11:1; 7-8, 11
- Saul - 1 Samuel 9:1-2
- David - 1 Samuel 17:11-12; 50-51
- Esther - Esther 2:7; 17, 8:8

CLASS ACTIVITY – Students should identify those qualities which helped the above-listed persons to become champions.

ii. *LESSON OUTLINE 2* – JESUS IS THE GREATEST CHAMPION

Jesus was valiant in the following accounts and as a result emerged the greatest champion at all times:

- He defeated the devil on various occasions. Gen. 3:15; Heb. 2:14-15.
- He conquered and established victory over sin. I Cor. 15:56-57; Rom. 8:3.
- He conquered the world and all its powers. John 16:3 3
- He conquered death in victory. I Cor. 15:54
- He won various battles for you. Romans 8:31-37

3. SUMMARY

The Bible contains long list of champions who were raised by God Almighty. Jesus is the all-times greatest champion and we too can become a champion through Jesus Christ.

4. CONCLUSION

If you are struggling with flesh, sin, host of darkness, etc. You should yield your life to the greatest champion and He will make you a champion, 1 John 4:4

5. ASSIGNMENT

Students should study how a champion could be made.

LESSON 33
DIVINE CHAMPION

PRAYER POINT – Father, grant to me strength and wisdom to become and remain a divine champion, in Jesus name.

PREVIOUS KNOWLEDGE – The Assistant Teacher should review the previous week's lesson with particular attention paid to the outlines, summary and conclusion.

TODAY'S LESSON

1. OPENING

i. **LESSON TEXT** – Daniel 2:1-5, 12-20

ii. **MEMORY VERSE** – "Behold thou desireth truth in the inward part and in the hidden part thou shall make me to know wisdom" Psalm 51:6

iii. **LESSON INTRODUCTION** – Last week we examined Jesus Christ as the greatest champion. We also learned that He became a champion to make you one also if you can accept Him as Lord and savior and follow Him. Today's topic will focus on the strength and wisdom of a champion.

TEACHER'S DIARY

i. **LESSON AIM** – To study what constitutes the strength and wisdom of a divine champion.

ii. **TEACHING OBJECTIVES AND LESSON PLAN** – After the lesson, students should be able to discover the strength and wisdom of a divine champion. Teacher should teach the two lesson outlines with relevant Biblical reference.

iii. ***TEXT REVIEW*** – Daniel 2:1-5; 12-20

"The gods are blind"

It may not be too difficult to interpret somebody's dream correctly. But when it comes to dreaming another person's dream and to give its interpretation, then it is beyond the knowledge of the gods. No wonder, the Chaldeans, sorcerer, magicians and astrologers said, "No man on earth can dream your dream". Dan. 2:10-11. But Daniel did not only dream the dream of the king, he went further to give the interpretation. How did this wonder happen? God revealed it to him in a night vision. Dan. 2:19-20. Few lessons are here to learn:

- The astrologers and magicians are inferior to our God.
- They are laden with failures and impossibilities.
- The magicians, herbalists and their oracles could not see or dream your dreams talk less of interpreting them, what a shame! Your future is not revealed to them in their visions.
- Only the Almighty God knows your dreams and destinies and can help you to interpret and realize them. Praise God!
- They do not own your destiny. Do not go to them.

iv. ***TEACHING METHOD*** – Teacher should combine question, lecture and discussion method.

v. ***TIME MANAGEMENT*** – Allocate time equally to the two lesson outlines.

2. LESSON OUTLINES

i. ***LESSON OUTLINE A*** – THE STRENGTH OF A DIVINE CHAMPION

- The Lord is the strength of the divine Champion. Psalm 27:1.

The provision of the Lord is the strength of the divine champion. I Kings 19:7-8

- Absolute faith in the powers of God strengthens the divine champion against fear and prevents him from falling. Psalm 27:1-2

- Whenever the divine champion is encumbered with troubles, reproaches, shame, distress, the strength of the Almighty God rejuvenates him to bounce back. 2 Corinthians 12:10
- God will always honor and back up the divine champions. I Kings 18:36; Dan. 3:16-18; 24-26

CLASS ACTIVITY – Each member of the class should mention one example of a divine champion in the Bible and what he/she did.

ii. *LESSON OUTLINE B* – THE WISDOM OF A DIVINE CHAMPION.
- The wisdom from above (The Almighty God) is the source of the wisdom of the divine champion. James 3:17; Dan. 2:20-21.
- Divine wisdom makes way for progress and success for the divine champion. Eccl. 10:10; I Sam. 3:19, Gen. 41:33-41.
- For divine champion not to lose his divine strength, wisdom and victories, he/she should run away from sin. Judges 16:28-30.

3. **SUMMARY**
The strength of the divine champion is God, the source of the wisdom of the divine champion is God and the secret behind the victories of the divine champions is God

4. **CONCLUSION**
To remain a divine champion, you must run away from every trace of sin Prov. 14:34.

5. **ASSIGNMENT**
Students should study the strength and wisdom of divine champion of a child of God

LESSON 34
HE WAS BETRAYED

PRAYER POINT – Pray against wolfs in sheep clothing's in the church. Ask God to reveal and expose betrayers in the body of Christ.

PREVIOUS KNOWLEDGE – Class teacher should review the previous week lessons with the students.

TODAY'S LESSON

1. OPENING

i. ***LESSON TEXT*** – Matthew 26:47-75

ii. ***MEMORY VERSE*** – "And while He was still speaking, behold, a multitude; and he who was called Judas, one of the twelve, went before them and drew near to Jesus to kiss Him." Luke 22:47

iii. ***LESSON INTRODUCTION*** – To betray is to be a traitor or to be disloyal. It is to disclose secret information. Jesus went through some serious negative aspects of life. He was betrayed, arrested and deserted. Some of the actions came from His close associates Apostles. Those He called, trusted and appointed to positions disappointed, when it mattered most. His three closest disciples slept off when it was time to watch in prayer, Matt. 26:36-46. Judas His treasurer betrayed him while Peter followed afar off, Mk. 14:54, and denied Him. It is our prayer that the Lord will teach us today in the name of Jesus Christ.

TEACHER'S DIARY

i. ***LESSON AIM*** – To learn from the betrayer of Jesus Christ our Lord.

ii. ***TEACHING OBJECTIVES AND LESSON PLAN*** – At the end of the lesson, students should be able to learn that not all Christians and friends are true, that holding grudges does not really solve one's problems and learn how to forgive and move on when one is betrayed. To achieve these objectives, teacher should explain both outlines as stated in the teacher's manual and allow students to participate in the class activities.

iii. ***TEXT REVIEW*** – Matthew 26:47-75
- Finally Judas comes and kisses Jesus. This is the signal to the chief priest and elders to arrest Jesus. Vs 47-49
- Out of protection, one of the disciples draws a sword and cuts the ear of a servant. Jesus tells him to the put the sword away because "all who take the sword will perish by the sword" Vs 51-52.
- Jesus is taken to be seen before Caiaphas, the high priest. Like a good little stalker, Peter follows at a distance. Vs 57
- The chief priests try to find people to testify against Jesus. Vs 59
- But then two people come forward saying that Jesus claimed he could destroy the temple and rebuild it in the three days. Vs 60-61
- When asked (under oath) if he is the Son of God, Jesus replies that they have said so. Then, for good measure, he quotes scripture. Vs 64
- The high priests accuse him of blasphemy and they begin to strike and taunt him. Vs 66-68
- Meanwhile, in the courtyard:Peter gets recognized as being friends with Jesus. He denies it not once, not twice, but three times. After the third denial, the cock crows. Vs 69-74
- Immediately Peter remembered Jesus's prediction. Vs 75

iv. ***TEACHING METHOD*** – Teacher should use discussion method. Review briefly the events that occurred in the Garden of Gethsemane and ask for lesson they will learn

v. ***TIME MANAGEMENT*** – Allocate time equally to the two lesson outlines.

CLASS ACTIVITY – Class should discuss how associations with ungodly can lead to betrayal.

2. LESSON OUTLINES

i. *LESSON OUTLINE 1* – WHY BETRAYAL IS POSSIBLE
- Those who betray are often close and friendly – Ps. 55:12; 41:9; Lam. 1:19.
- People who betray have intimate relationship, like husband and wife. Judas ate with Jesus Christ, Mk.14:18.
- He could betray with a kiss because of the intimacy, Matt. 26:49. Jesus even called him friend, Matt. 26:50.
- Motives could include an expectation of personal gain. Remember the comments of Judas in John 12:6 and Matthew 26:9.
- A lot could be concealed, Judas went about the betrayal in the night, Jn. 13:30.
- A lot of plans are carried out in the heart of man before it becomes manifested in action, Pro. 19:21

ii. *LESSON OUTLINE 2*: INAPPROPRIATE ASSOCIATION
- How did Judas come to be with the multitude?
- Think of the effects of associations with ungodly, Ps. 1:1-6; 2 Cor. 6:14-18.
- They came with weapons, swords and clubs, Matt. 26:47.
- What are the weapons of mass destruction of Jesus Christ, leaders and other brethren today?
- Consider the position of mouth and tongues in many brethren, Rom. 3:13-17.
- Consider that Judas and the multitude came from the Chief Priests and elders of the people.
- Judas even gave them a sign of a kiss, Matt. 26:49. In what areas are people only religious without much commitment to the master?
- Jesus Christ said that people draw near Him with their mouth without commitment from the heart, Matt. 15:8.
- Jesus Christ some religious people "brood of vipers", Matt. 12:34. Are there children of God in this category today?

3. **SUMMARY**

   Judas one of the closest Apostle of our Lord Jesus Christ eat the last meal in the same plate with him. Shortly after he betrayed him to his enemies for 30 shekels of sliver and a kiss.

4. **CONCLUSION**

   It is possible to be in the church today and still betray the master. Betrayal could be gradual and this include inappropriate relationship with unfruitful works of darkness. It is better to watch your friendship and what you say with your tongue. It is better to identify the process of betrayal quit before it happens. If you have gone into it, go back to God today. Judas Iscariot repented to the Chief Priests and elders not to Jesus Christ. The end was suicide, Matt. 27:3-5

LESSON 35
WHEN GOD ASKS QUESTIONS

PRAYER POINT – The entire class should pray for wisdom to answer effectively

PREVIOUS KNOWLEDGE – Class teacher should review the previous week lessons with the students.

TODAY'S LESSON

1. OPENING

i. ***LESSON TEXT*** – 2 Sam:12:1-9

ii. ***MEMORY VERSE*** – "He asked me, "Son of man, can these bones live?" I said, "Sovereign Lord, you alone know." Ezek. 37:3

iii. ***LESSON INTRODUCTION*** – It is normal when human beings ask one another questions when there are situations beyond their understanding. They turn to God. "Why me?" is one of the many questions. Do you know that the longest list of questions found in the Bible is made up of questions asked by God? Why would God who is omnipotent (Rev 19:6) ask human beings who are mortals' questions. Why would Alpha and Omega with whom nothing is impossible and knows the end before the beginning (Lk. 18:27; Lk. 1:37, Rev. 1:8) ask questions. When God who knows a man before he was born, Jer. 1:5, asks questions they cannot be ignored. It is our prayer that the Almighty God will teach us today in the name of Jesus Christ. Amen

TEACHER'S DIARY

i. ***LESSON AIM*** – To teach the students about how God asked what should be done when God asks questions.

ii. **TEACHING OBJECTIVES AND LESSON PLAN** – At the end of the lesson, students should be able to, know some questions God asked in time past, check what would be their response if they were ask similar questions and be ready to answer God's questions positively, whenever and wherever. To achieve these objectives, teacher should explain both outlines as stated in the teacher's manual and allow students to participate in the class activities.

iii. **TEXT REVIEW** – 2 Sam:12:1-9

- God sent Prophet Nathan to David when He wanted to ask him question.1Sam12:1-4
- David pronounced judgement without listening to the question God was about to ask him? 1 Sam 12:4-6
- Nathan revealed the evil and murder David committed.
- What David did was despicable and despising to God.

iv. **TEACHING METHOD** – Teacher should use discussion method.

v. **TIME MANAGEMENT** – Allocate time equally to the two lesson outlines.

2. LESSON OUTLINES

i. **LESSON OUTLINE A** – SOME QUESTIONS BY GOD 2 Sam 12:1-9

- God asked Adam "Where art thou?" Gen. 3:9. This is the first question God asks in the Bible. God is still asking sinners the same question today.
- God asked, "Who told you that you were naked" Gen 3:10. Nobody had to tell them they were naked. Whenever we sin, our conscience will condemn us.1 John 3:21.
- God asked Cain, "Where is thy brother?", Gen. 4:19
- God asked Moses, "What is that you have in your hand?" Ex. 4
- God asked David, "Why did you do it? 2 Sam. 12:9
- God asked Ezekiel, "Can these bones live?" Ezek. 37:3

- God asked Malachi, "Will a man rob God?" Mal. 3:8
- God asked blind Bartholomew "What do you want me to do for you?", Mk. 10:53
- God asked a lame man, "Wilt thou be made whole?" John 5:6

ii. *LESSON OUTLINE B* – SOME ANSWERS
- God does not ask questions because He doesn't know the answers. He asks us deep, penetrating questions because He wants us to think.
- When God asks us a question, we really need to sit up and pay attention. Is 1:18.
- He introduced Himself to Abraham as the Almighty, Gen. 17:1a, questions like "Is there anything too hard for God?" presupposed that God did not ask the question for knowledge.
- He knows all things. Like Ezekiel replied in Ezekiel 37:3, "O Lord God, You Know."
- God is a God of purpose and has reasons for every questions He asked.
- Gen 3:9-13. Why would God ask all those involved, Adam, Eve, and the Serpent, questions?
- Think of the question, "Adam, where are you?". Was God asking the question as it relates to location?
- Think of these questions: Where are you after the devil has finished with you? Where are you after giving in to disobedience?
- Are you still in the position of dominion and authority where I placed you? Are you better now than before?
- Why are you not in our regular meeting place? Are you running away thinking you can cover your shame with fig leaves?
- We can add our thoughts to the questions.
- 2 Samuel 12:9- "Why have you despised the commandments of the Lord to do evil in His sight?" what are some other interpretations of this question? Think of the message of the Lord through Prophet Nathan in verse 7 and 8.

ii. ***LESSON OUTLINE C*** – OUR PLACE IN THE TWO QUESTIONS
- Is God asking us these questions today?
- If God asks you "Where Art Thou?" Where are you in the journey of life? Where are you in tolerance? Humility? Anger? Managing the resources of God at your disposal?
- How relevant is the question, "Wherefore hast thou despised the commandment of the Lord to do evil in His sight"

CLASS ACTIVITY – Teacher should select a student to represent God who will ask others questions.

3. SUMMARY
When God asks question, It is to raise man's awareness and not because he does not know the answer.

4. CONCLUSION
Our responses when God is scrutinizing, matters a lot. It matters much if we cooperate with the Holy Spirit. It is our prayers that a meaningful positive response takes place today in the Name of Jesus Christ. Amen

5. ASSIGNMENT
Students should study God's question to Hagar in Gen. 29:17 – "What hails you Hagar?"

LESSON 36
ANGELS

PRAYER POINT – Ask the Lord to open your understanding to discover the truth of His word in the lesson of today.

PREVIOUS KNOWLEDGE – The teacher asks students to enumerate the facts they studied about the Holy Spirit during the previous lesson.

TODAY'S LESSON

1. OPENING

   i. ***LESSON TEXT*** – Psalm 91:1-16.

   ii. ***MEMORY VERSE*** – "For He shall give His angels charge over you, to keep you in all your ways." Psalm 91:11

   iii. ***LESSON INTRODUCTION*** – We know little about the angels, their nature, their population, their duties, their position, and the believer's relationship with them. Today's lesson will shed more light on some of the questions that agitate our minds about the angels.

TEACHER'S DIARY

   i. ***LESSON AIM*** – To know more about Angels.

   ii. ***LESSON AIM AND TEACHING OBJECTIVE*** – To study about the angels and at the end of the lesson, students should be able to describe who the angels are, their population as well as their roles.

   iii. ***TEXT REVIEW*** – Psalm 91:1-16
   - The text exposes us to the mighty power possessed by the angels of the Lord. This power can control the lion, serpent, dragon, and

terror by night, arrow that flies in the day, pestilence, darkness and destruction - vs. 13, 5-6.

- They are to exercise their powers on behalf of the children of God for their safety and absolute security - vs. 11.
- Whenever angels of God discharge these responsibilities of taking charge, no evil would befall the believer - vs. 10.
- If the angels strike, tens of thousands of the enemies of God's children would be wasted - vs. 7.

Key note - We should be grateful to God for creating His holy angels to take care of believers in all our ways.

iv. *TEACHING METHOD* – Use lecture method.

v. *TIME MANAGEMENT* – Allocate time equally to the four lesson outlines.

2. LESSON OUTLINES

i. *LESSON OUTLINE A* – THE NATURE OF ANGELS
- They are spirit beings - Hebrews 1:14.
- Human laws do not bind them.
- They cannot be locked in or out - Acts 12:7.
- They can cover a great distance within a few seconds.
- Fire or water has no influence on them - Judges 13:19-20.
- They are wise and intelligent.
- They are very strong - Psalm 103:20.
- They are champions in battle. One angel can destroy a great number of enemies in battle - 2 Kings 19:35; 2 Sam. 24:15-16.
- They can break chains and iron doors. They can roll away great stones or barriers.
- They can blindfold or bring havoc to evil people.
- They are immortal - Luke 20:35-36.
- They are highly organized in hierarchical order.

ii. ***LESSON OUTLINE B*** – THEIR NUMBER
- They are very many - Rev. 5:11.
- They are more than twelve legion - Matt. 26:53.
- They are innumerable - Hebrews 12:22.

iii. ***LESSON OUTLINE C*** – DUTIES OF ANGELS
- They honor, worship and serve God in Heaven - Rev. 5:11-12.
- They minister to the needs of God's people.
- They execute God's judgment on earth, for instance:
    - An angel blocked Balaam from cursing the Israelites - Numbers 22:22.
    - An angel struck and killed the wicked king Herod - Acts 12:23.
    - Angels will cast the sinful tares (the ungodly) into fire at the last judgment - Matt. 13:41.
- Angels provide security (guards) to the believers, for instance:
    - They shut the mouths of lions from killing Daniel - Daniel 6:22.
    - Angels prevented Peter from being executed.
- Angels provide strength to believers when they are weak - Luke 22:43.
- They guide us to work for God - Acts 8:26.
- They will herald the Lord's coming - Matt. 25:31.
- They will take believers to Heaven after death - Luke 16:22.
- They will bind the devil and cast him into the bottomless pit - Rev. 20:1-3.
- They would cast the devil into the lake of fire - Rev. 20:10.

iv. ***LESSON OUTLINE D*** – THE SUPERIOR, MAN / ANGELS
- By creation, Man is made a little lower than the angels - Psalm 8:5.
- By death, Man is made lesser than the angels for angels are immortal.

- Through the grace of the Lord, angels are made to be ministers unto us (the born again Christians) -Hebrews 1:14.
- Believers will judge the angels - 1 Cor. 6:3.
- God, through His mercy, has put all things under Man and has made him have dominion over His work - Psalm 8:6.

3. SUMMARY

Angels are spirit beings formed by God. They perform some wonderful functions for God and for God's children. Those angels that sinned along with Satan would be judged and be cast into darkness while the holy angels would abide with the Lord forever - Jude 1:6,14.

4. CONCLUSION

God created the angels for His purpose.

5. ASSIGNMENT

Students should distinguish between man and angels, using appropriate scriptures where necessary.

LESSON 37
LUCIFER

PRAYER POINT – Pray for the grace and power not to fall prey into the hands of Satan (Lucifer)

PREVIOUS KNOWLEDGE The teacher reviews the lesson of the previous week. The teacher asks students to summarize their findings from the take home assignment.

TODAY'S LESSON

1. OPENING

i. ***LESSON TEXT*** – Ezekiel 28:12-19; Isaiah 14:12-17

ii. ***MEMORY VERSE*** – "Hereafter I will not talk much with you: for the prince of this world cometh, and hath nothing in me," John 14:30.

iii. ***LESSON INTRODUCTION*** – Every regenerated person is in a great trouble with Satan. This is so because he or she has to engage in constant combat with the devil in order to maintain victories over the devil. Any simple relaxation turns such a believer captive in the prison of Satan.

TEACHER'S DIARY

i. ***LESSON AIM*** – To study about Lucifer.

ii. ***LESSON AIM*** AND TEACHING OBJECTIVE – To study the identity and duties of Lucifer with a view to overcome his tricks. At the end of the lesson, students should be able to describe the personality and identity of Satan as well as his works. They should also be able to discover how to overcome his wicked plans for humanity.

iii. ***TEXT REVIEW*** – Ezekiel 28:12-19; Isaiah 14:12-17.

Most of the paintings around us present the devil as an ugly being. This is not true.
- The devil is very perfect in beauty - Ezek. 28:12.
- He is exceptionally brilliant and full of wisdom - vs. 12, 17.
- He was not made of blood and flesh but of precious stones and gold - vs. 13.
- He is made up of pipes and all forms of musical instruments - vs. 13.
- He was once highly anointed by God - vs. 14.
- He was once upon the mountain of God - vs. 14.
- He was proud and became disrespectful to God - Ezek. 28:16-17; Isaiah 14:13-14.
- After he was cast down to earth, he became very violent - vs. 16.
- The devil is very corrupt - vs. 17.
- The devil is the chief sinner - vs. 18.

Consequent upon these evil natures of the devil, the Lord will not let him go free. He would be judged and burnt into ashes - vs. 18-19.

NOTE: Teacher can use these points to support lesson outline 2.

iv. ***TEACHING METHOD*** – Use discussion teaching method.

v. ***TIME MANAGEMENT*** – Allocate time equally to the five lesson outlines.

2. LESSON OUTLINES

i. ***LESSON OUTLINE A*** – THE ORIGIN OF SATAN
- His origin on earth can be traced to when he appeared in the Garden of Eden - Ezek. 28:13; Genesis 3:1.
- He was once upon the holy mountain of God being fully anointed before he sinned and was cast down into the earth - Ezek. 28:14.

- Before he was cast down from Heaven to the earth, he was perfect in all his ways - Ezek. 28:14.
- Presently, the devil roams the earth and has his headquarters in the air - Job 2:1-2; Ephesians 2:2.
- He is not afraid of mingling with the children of God to accuse them before the Lord - Job 1:6-12; Zechariah 3:1.

KEY NOTE: Satan is a restless wanderer.

ii. ***LESSON OUTLINE B*** – THE NATURE OF SATAN
- Satan is beautiful.
- Satan is very brilliant and extremely intelligent.
- Satan is subtle - 2 Cor. 11:13.
- Satan is a thief - Matt. 13:19.
- Satan is a liar - John 8:44.

QUESTION: What are the implications of the above for Christian living?

- He uses his beauty to entice men and women into fornication and adultery.
- Being very subtle, he deceives people easily.
- Being a thief, Satan steals people's health, joy, success, wealth and worst of all, the relationship between man and God.
- Being a liar, he corrupts the truth. He defiles the truth.
- Being a murderer, he constantly fulfills his threefold ministry of stealing, killing and destroying - John 10:10.

KEY NOTE: Christians have to be watchful, absolutely.

iii. ***LESSON OUTLINE C*** – HIS OTHER TITLES
- He was described as an angel of light - 2 Cor. 11:14.
- He was described as a roaring lion - 1 Pet. 5:8.
- Satan was the prince of power of the air - Eph. 2:2.
- He is the coordinator of the powers of darkness such as cultism, witchcraft, sorcery, and all evil fraternities - Col. 1:13.
- He is the dragon, serpent, and the devil - Rev. 12:9.

- He is the prince of this world - John 14:30.
- He is the god of this world - 2 Cor. 4:4.
- He is the king of the bottomless pit.
- He is Abaddon, - Rev. 9:11.

QUESTION: Why do we need to know his title?

- To get off from the hook of his tricks.
- He is not the real lion but like it.
- To enable us avoid him and his domains.
- To enable us identify the powers at play.
- To equip us to be battle ready for him.

iv. *LESSON OUTLINE D* – HIS DUTIES

- It is very wrong for a Christian to think that God does or tempts with evil.
- Whatever is good comes from God and whatever is evil comes from the devil.
- He kills.
- He deceives.
- He devours.
- He accuses.
- He blindfolds and so on.

Apply scriptures appropriately:1 Pet. 5:8; 1 Cor. 5:5; Matt. 13:25, 30; 2 Cor. 4:4; Luke 22:31.

CLASS ACTIVITY - Students may identify other duties of Satan.

v. *LESSON OUTLINE E* – HIS DESTINY

- The Lord will cut short his nefarious activities by sending down His angel to bind him and cast him down into the bottomless pit - Rev. 20:1-3.
- He would finally be cast into the lake of fire forever - Rev. 20:7-10.
- Lucifer, his agents and his false prophets would be tormented day and night for ever - Rev. 20:10

3. **SUMMARY**

   From the creation of the world, the devil has really struck the earth hard and has painted the world red with all forms of evils thereby fulfilling his ministry. However, his end is near when he would be bound in chains and cast into the lake of fire in torment forever. Then Christ's Kingdom of peace would be established.

4. **CONCLUSION**

   Since Christ has defeated the devil, let us claim our victories over him

5. **ASSIGNMENT**

   Do something quickly about the devil's kingdom. You may ask the Holy Spirit to teach you

LESSON 38
THAT I MAY KNOW HIM

PRAYER POINT – Father, met me know you daily and the power of your resurrection and the fellowship of your suffering, in Jesus name. Amen.

PREVIOUS KNOWLEDGE – Teacher should allow the students to review the previous week's lesson through guided questions which focus on Memory Verse, Lesson Outline, Class Activities and Summary.

TODAY'S LESSON

1. **OPENING**

    i. ***LESSON TEXT*** – Philippians 3:1-11

    ii. ***MEMORY VERSE*** – "That I may know him, and the power of his resurrection, and the fellowship of his sufferings, being made conformable unto his death" Philippians 3:10

    iii. ***LESSON INTRODUCTION*** – Paul displayed seven credentials in Phil.3:1-11, of which he gained by birth and three by his own action:"circumcised on the eighth day." He was no convert to Judaism who would have been circumcised later, but was born into it. "of the people of Israel." He was not a Gentile, but a Jew. "of the tribe of Benjamin." The tribe of Benjamin was small, but prominent in that the first king of Israel was from this tribe -- Saul, after whom Paul was named. "a Hebrew of Hebrews." Unlike Jewish proselytes, he spoke Hebrew and Aramaic and was the son of a family that did so. "in regard to the law, a Pharisee." He had been a strict Pharisee, educated at the feet of Gamaliel, a highly respected rabbi. Acts 5:34-40; 22:3. "as for zeal, persecuting the church." He had been so zealous for orthodox, Pharisaical Judaism that he had persecuted the church. Acts 9:1-2. "as for legalistic righteousness, faultless. Despite the achievements of Paul, he was desperately longing and yearning to know God. In this eloquent passage we heard his heart's cry for God, a prayer that all believers must pray along with him. "I want to know Christ!" Phil. 3:7-9a.

TEACHER'S DIARY

i. ***LESSON AIM*** – To study how to know Christ, and the power of His resurrection and the fellowship of His suffering.

ii. ***TEACHING OBJECTIVES AND TEACHING PLAN*** – After the lesson, students should be able to understand what it means to know Christ and understand how to know Him. Teacher should summarize, conclude and evaluate the lesson. Teacher should also give assignment to students from the work book.

iii ***TEXT REVIEW*** – Philippians 3:1-11

BEWARE OF DOGS!

Dogs are domestic animals with various degrees of usefulness. For instance; there are sporting dogs, e.g. Retriever; herding dogs, e.g. German shepherd; hounds, e.g. Beagle; toy dogs e.g Poodle; working dogs e.g Rottweiler, Bull dog; etc. Some are so friendly while others are not. Some of them enjoy certain degrees of rights and privileges and exhibit some level of intelligence, etc. However, dogs are animals and not man. God did not give dominion to animals but to man. Similarly in today's Bible Passage, God warned believers against men who exhibit behavior of dogs:

- Dogs live in the house but most of them sleep outside the house or better still, in various cages. Rev. 22:15.
- Many dogs eat the crumbs from the table and not the real food. Matt. 15:26-27.
- Many dogs return to their vomit being greedy. Isaiah 56:11.
- Many of them are noise makers and wicked. Psalm 22:16
- People with these characters are in the church. They do not know Christ and have no part in the kingdom.
- They must quickly repent or else genuine believers must beware/ run away from them. Philippians 3:2. This is a serious warning!

iv. **TEACHING METHOD** – Teacher should use the lecture teaching method.

v. **TIME MANAGEMENT** – Allocate time equally to the two lesson outlines.

2. LESSON OUTLINES

i. ***LESSON OUTLINE A*** – WHAT IT MEAN TO 'KNOW' CHRIST
- To know means to live in a close relationship with something or somebody.
- To know Christ therefore means to live in a close relationship with Christ.
- It also means to have communion (fellowship with Christ). Isaiah 11:9
- It also means to develop a close personal relationship with Christ. Isaiah 11:9; Matthew 15:8; 2 Chronicle 15:2

CLASS ACTIVITY – Account for reasons why people pretend to know Christ when in actual fact they do not know Him.

ii. ***LESSON OUTLINE B*** – HOW TO KNOW HIM
You and I can know Christ through the following means:
- Through the fear and reverence of God. Prov.1:7, 2:1-5.
- Through genuine demonstration of love. 1 Jn.4:7-8
- Through intimacy prompted by God and pursued by men. Ps.103:7; Mk.3:14-15; Ps.27:4
- Through worship by the Spirit of God. John 4:21, 23 Spiritual worship is prayer, praise, and a life lived in dedication to God.
- By putting no confidence in the flesh. "Flesh" is referring to both physical circumcision and sinful human nature as opposed to spiritual obedience to God. Phil.3:3
- By yielding to the Holy Spirit who can reveal to us the very mind of Christ. 1 Cor.2:16; Jn.16:13.

- ✳ ○ Through His word, through prayer, to become Christ-like ourselves. 2Tim.2:15; 1 Chr.16:11; Prov.28:5.

3. **SUMMARY**
   We must have close relationship and communion with Christ daily through fear of God, love of God, worship in truth, etc.

4. **CONCLUSION**
   Before we can develop a relationship at that level, we must have faith in Christ. Without faith, he will be a mere acquaintance, and His power will not be seen in our life. Conversely, if we aren't seeking a personal relationship with Christ, our "faith" is empty.

5. **ASSIGNMENT**
   Student should study what Sunday School could do to enable people know Christ.

LESSON 39

THE THIRD QUARTER INTERACTIVE SESSION

Welcome to the third interactive session

Your privileges:

- To ask questions on treated lessons for clarity
- To give critical appraisal of the outline
- To give useful suggestions towards better performance
- To give useful spiritual contributions

LESSON 40
FELLOWSHIP WITH OTHERS

PRAYER POINT – Father, help, the members of our church to consider fellowshipping together as paramount, in Jesus name.

PREVIOUS KNOWLEDGE – Teacher should review the previous week's lesson.

TODAY'S LESSON

1. OPENING

i. ***LESSON TEXT*** – Acts 2:44-47

ii. ***MEMORY VERSE*** – "And let us consider one another to provoke unto love and to good works". Hebrews 10:24

iii. ***LESSON INTRODUCTION*** – There has always been a crucial need for relational interaction among Christians alike. For it to be meaningful and beneficial, it must go beyond the realms of preaching, teaching, fasting, studying and praise/worship. It must be full of deep felt concern and care for the emotional and physical well-being of one another in the household of God. Effective fellowship is having a heart to rejoice with and a shoulder to cry on. Rom. 12:15.

TEACHER'S DIARY

i. ***LESSON AIM*** – To study the significance of fellowshipping together in the church.

ii. TEACHING OBJECTIVES AND TEACHING PLAN – At the end of the lesson, students should be able to understand the meaning and importance of Christian fellowship and the benefits of genuine Christian fellowship. Teacher should allow the students to take the opening prayer, read the Bible Passage, recite the memory verse, do the class activities and the assignment.

iii. **TEXT REVIEW** – Acts 2:44-47

The following elements of fellowshipping are apparent in today's Bible Passage.

- Togetherness/Interaction Acts 2:44
- Commonality. Acts 2:.44
- Generosity. Acts 2:45
- Continuity. Acts 2:47
- Agreement Acts 2:44
- Communion & Communication Acts 2:46
- Celebration/Jubilation. Acts 2:46
- Oneness. Acts 2:46
- Singspiration. Acts 2:47
- Multiplication. Acts 2:47
- Salvation. Acts 2:47

If the above elements of true fellowshipping are present in our services at all times, our services/ fellowshipping will be glorious, miraculous and full of over flowing blessings.

iv. **TEACHING METHOD** – Teacher should use lecture teaching method.

v. **TIME MANAGEMENT** – Allocate time equally to the two lesson outlines.

2. LESSON OUTLINES

i. **LESSON OUTLINE A** – MEANING AND IMPORTANCE OF CHRISTIAN FELLOWSHIP
- Spending time with each other in sharing and learning. Christians should have spiritual fellowship with God and man.

- Christians should not forsake fellowshipping with one another. Heb. 10:25; Psalm 133:1-3
- Christians should interact in all areas of life which include the physical, emotional and physiological needs.
- Christian fellowship helps to discover the strength and weaknesses of other Christians without being judgmental. Romans 14:1
- Through Christian fellowship, believer's challenges and rejoicing are tackled or celebrated together. Proverb. 27:17
- Christian fellowship must be devoid of selfishness and ulterior motive.

CLASS ACTIVITY – What can the Sunday school do to ensure that all its members/students attend the House Fellowship or fellowship constantly in every service?

ii. ***LESSON OUTLINE B*** – BENEFITS OF GENUINE CHRISTIAN FELLOWSHIP

The overall benefits of genuine Christian fellowship can be summarized as follows:
- An atmosphere to share personal day to day experiences and learn from each other. Philemon 1-2
- Personal growth and accountability. Gal.6:1-2
- Support for crucial family needs e.g. childcare, job opportunities, business ideas and important information. Gal.6:10
- Effective mentoring to avert negative worldly influence. 1 Tim. 6:17-18, Rom. 14:1
- Provides ample support and encouragement in times of adversity. Col. 2:2, Heb. 13:16

3. **SUMMARY**

Fellowship with man can be described as interaction through meeting, program, and services or with each or one another. Fellowship with God is worship or devotion, while fellowshipping with man and God brings unimaginable benefits which cannot be overemphasised.

4. CONCLUSION
The household of God should be a safe haven for support and encouragement in times of need. All efforts must be geared to making adequate provisions for the spiritual as well as the physical needs of the worshippers within the confines of the church in line with the will of God.

5. ASSIGNMENT
Students should study how we can improve our fellowship with God the Father, Son and Holy.

LESSON 41
RAPE

PRAYER POINT – Father, do not give me over to a reprobate mind, in Jesus name.

PREVIOUS KNOWLEDGE – The Assistant Teacher should review the previous week's lesson.

TODAY'S LESSON

1. OPENING

i. ***LESSON TEXT*** – Deuteronomy 22:25-27

ii. ***MEMORY VERSE*** – "And even as they did not like to retain God in their knowledge, God gave them over to a reprobate mind, to do those things which are not convenient;" Romans 1:28

iii. ***LESSON INTRODUCTION*** – According to World Health Organization:Rape is an act of forcing someone to have sex when he/she is unwilling. It is also a type of sexual assault usually involving sexual intercourse or other forms of sexual abuse initiated against one or more individual without the consent of those individuals. The act may be carried out by physical force, coercion, abuse of authority or against a person who is incapable of valid consent, such as one who is unconscious, incapacitated or below the legal age of consent.

TEACHER'S DIARY

i. ***LESSON AIM*** – To study some causes and consequences of rape and comfort to victims.

ii. TEACHING OBJECTIVES AND TECHING PLAN – After the lesson, students should be able to discover some types and causes of rape and understand consequences and comfort to the victims. Teacher should allow the Assistant Teacher to review the previous week's lesson and introduce the lesson.

iii. ***TEXT REVIEW*** – Deuteronomy 22:25-27

The law of the Lord is very clear on the issue of rape:
- The rapist shall die. Deut. 22:25
- The Damsel shall live. Deut. 22:26-27. Provided she cried for help.
- Rape a sin worth of death. Deut.22:26.
- Whoredom and Prostitution carry the same penalty of death. Deut.22:21
- Those playing or scheming or luring other people's wives or fiancés for benefit of sexual advantage are playing with death. Deut.22:24
- Those who have ears should better listen!

iv. ***TEACHING METHOD*** – Teacher should use the lecture teaching method.

v. ***TIME MANAGEMENT*** – Allocate time equally to the three lesson outlines.

2. LESSON OUTLINES

i. ***LESSON OUTLINE A*** – TYPES OF CAUSES
- Marital rape – This is rape committed by the person to whom the victim is married. It is also unwanted sexual acts by a spouse Eph. 5:22; 1Cor. 7:1-5
- Gang rape – This is the rape of one person by a group of other people. Judges 19:22-25.
- Child rape – This is a form of child abuse in which an adult or older adolescent uses a child for illicit sexual satisfaction or other purposes. Matt. 18:6.

- Incest rape – Incest is sexual activity between family members or close relatives. Gen. 19:33-35; 2Sam. 13:10-14.
- War rape – During war and armed conflict, rape is frequently used as a means of psychological warfare in order to humiliate the enemies. Zech. 14:2.
- Other types of rape include prison rape, acquaintance rape and date rape, etc.

ii. ***LESSON OUTLINE B* – CAUSES OF RAPE**
- Indecent dressing: Dressing in a way that is likely to seduce. That is, wearing dresses that reveal nakedness or provoke undue attention. Phil. 4:9; 1Tim. 2:9-10.
- Bad company: Moving with people of negative influence Prov. 13:20; 2Sam. 13:3-5.
- Exposure to immoral acts through multi-media facilities e.g. Television, Magazines, Internet, cellphone etc.
- For fetish purposes: inordinate love of money or power in certain parts of the world can lead to the rape of innocent beings for fetish reasons. 1 Tim. 6:10.
- Lust: As a result of lust many have gone into this act, 2 Sam. 13:1-2.
- Idleness: this occurs when there is nothing to be done that is worthy of time or effort. There is a saying that "an idle hand is the devil's workshop". Prov. 21:25

CLASS ACTIVITY – Why do we have high incidence of rape in our modern society?

iii. ***LESSON OUTLINE C*– CONSEQUENCES TO THE VICTIMS**
THE CONSEQUENCES OF RAPE INCLUDE:
- Shame, Stigmatization and traumatization. 2 Sam. 13:19-20.
- Infection with sexually transmitted diseases (STD) such as HIV/AIDS, Gonorrhea, Syphilis, etc.
- Unwanted Pregnancy.
- Death may occur as a result of the above stated.

COMFORT FOR VICTIMS OF RAPE:

- Recourse to God for healing. God can heal all psychological, emotional trauma and related consequences of rape. Jeremiah 17:14; Psalm 147:3.
- Victim should forgive the rapist. Matthew 6:14.
- Victim should seek godly counsel. Pro. 15:22; Psalm 119:50.
- Victim should seek prompt/immediate medical treatment.

3. SUMMARY
These are examples of rape in the Bible such as incest rape, 2 Sam. 13:1-14, etc and every rape has its consequences upon the victim. However, the word of God provides comforts to the victim.

4. CONCLUSION
Rape is an act that defiles the body which is the temple of God and whosoever defiles God's temple shall be destroyed. 1 Cor. 3:17.

5. ASSIGNMENT
Students should study how the Church can help to reduce stigmatization on our society.

LESSON 42
ABORTION

PRAYER POINT – Father, help your church to live a life devoid of sin, in Jesus name.

PREVIOUS KNOWLEDGE – The Assistant Teacher should review the previous week's lesson with particular attention to the lesson outlines, summary and conclusion.

TODAY'S LESSON

1. **OPENING**

    i. ***LESSON TEXT*** – Genesis 1:26-2

    ii. ***MEMORY VERSE*** – "Ye have heard that it was said by them of old time, thou shalt not kill; and whosoever shall kill shall be in danger of the judgment" Matthew 5:21.

    iii. ***LESSON INTRODUCTION*** – Every seed planted in the womb of a woman is a blessing from God waiting for the time and place of manifestation. This seed refers to a new life that begins at conception. Therefore, every abortion ends (kills) the life of an innocent human being. Exodus 20:13.

TEACHER'S DIARY

   i. ***LESSON AIM*** – The study aims at discovering the reasons, consequences and the biblical position on abortion.

   ii. TEACHING OBJECTIVES AND TEACHING PLAN – At the end of the lesson, students should be able to discover the common reasons for abortion and the consequences and understand the biblical stand points on abortion. Teacher should teach the two lesson outlines with illustrations, from the Bible, summarize, conclude and evaluate the lesson.

iii. ***TEXT REVIEW*** – Genesis 1:26-28

The first two fundamental reasons why God created man in form of male and female are:

- For fruitfulness and
- For multiplication

Other three reasons are for replenishment, to subdue and for dominion. Man was commanded to extend the human race through family relationship of raising Godly children who will also propagate human existence until they have dominion on the whole earth.

God could not have commanded human being to multiply if he had supported abortion which is a form of killing of innocent lives.

iv. ***TEACHING METHOD*** – Teacher should use the lecture teaching method.

v. ***TIME MANAGEMENT*** – Allocate time equally to the two lesson outlines.

2. LESSON OUTLINES

i. ***LESSON OUTLINE A*** – COMMON REASONS FOR ABORTION

Reasons for abortion include:

- Unwanted pregnancy resulting from:
    - Extra-marital affairs – David and Bathsheba. 2Sam. 11:1-5.
    - Rape – Ammon and Tamar. 2 Sam. 13:10-14.
    - Incest – Judah and His daughter-in-law. Gen. 38:13-18.
    - Fornication i.e. sexual relations among unmarried people.
- Birth control – Married couples now use this as an excuse to terminate pregnancies. Often times, this is as a result of lack of finances or other reasons to cater for the unborn child.

- ○ Health challenges – When the life of the pregnant woman is at risk, it may be medically advisable to terminate such pregnancy to save the life of the woman.

  ii. ***LESSON OUTLINE B*** – THE CONSEQUENCES

  The consequences of abortion may include:

  - ○ Damages to the womb.
  - ○ Untimely death. Jas. 1:15; Rom. 1:28-32.
  - ○ Guilt and shame. Isa. 47:1-3.
  - ○ Separation from God. Isa. 59:1-3.
  - ○ God's wrath and judgments. Matt. 5:21; Col 3:5-6.

CLASS ACTIVITY – Class should discuss remedy for sexual sins which is prevalent in our society.

  iii. ***LESSON OUTLINE C*** – BIBLICAL STANDPOINTS ON ABORTION
  - ○ God commands us not to kill. Ex. 20:13.
  - ○ It is also a command of God that man should be fruitful and multiply on the surface of the earth. Gen. 1:28.
  - ○ Children are the heritage of God and blessings from Him. Ps. 127:3.
  - ○ Children from God are source(s) of Joy to man and not sorrow Ps. 127:5a.
  - ○ Every child no matter the issues surrounding the conception has a destiny to fulfill. Jer. 1:5; Matt. 1:18-21.

3. SUMMARY

Abortion is prevalent in our modern society and so many reasons are advanced for abortion. Yet, biblical point of view did not support it.

4. CONCLUSION

Since poverty, rape, health challenges and other circumstances are not sufficient reasons to justify the killing of human beings after birth, they are not also sufficient to justify the killing of human beings before birth.

5. ASSIGNMENT
Students should study how incidences of abortion can be controlled.

LESSON 43
PREPARING FOR MARRIAGE

PRAYER POINT – Let the class pray for all youths who are looking up for marriage to make the right choice that will glorify God, in the name of Jesus Christ.

PREVIOUS KNOWLEDGE – Teacher should allow the students to review the previous week's lesson through guided questions on the Memory Verse, Lesson Outlines, Summary and Conclusion.

TODAY'S LESSON

1. OPENING

i. ***LESSON TEXT*** – Genesis 2:22-25

ii. ***MEMORY VERSE*** – "And the LORD God said, It is not good that the man should be alone; I will make him a help meet for him" Genesis 2:18

iii. ***LESSON INTRODUCTION*** – Marriage preparation is not the same thing as wedding preparation. Wedding preparation is planning towards the ceremony while marriage preparation is planning towards the future of the couple. It also involves correct connection of a man and woman that God has ordained together for a blissful marital journey, Gen. 2:23.

TEACHER'S DIARY

i. ***LESSON AIM*** – To study on the basic preparations for marriage.

ii. ***TEACHING OBJECTIVES AND LESSON PLAN*** – At the end of the lesson, students should be able to understand the basic preparations for marriage. They should understand the need for right choice of partner in marriage. To achieve these objectives, students should be allowed to actively participate in the class. Teacher should teach the two lesson outlines and thereafter summarize and conclude the lesson. He should give assignment.

iii. **TEXT REVIEW** – Genesis 2:22-25

God's model of marriage is explained in a unified bond or structure that cannot be separated. The bond is explained in the following terms:

- God made woman from the rib He took from man. V.22
- Adam identified that the woman is her bone- the missing rib. V23.
- Man was incomplete until the rib is located and returned to man, "and brought her to the man." V.22
- The bond is further strengthened by the two words "leave" and "cleave". V.24
- Though we see a man and a woman in the natural, God sees one flesh in the spiritual. V.24
- No normal person (1 person) is ashamed of being alone, naked. The Man and wife were not ashamed because they were considered as one person who is not ashamed of seeing his or her own nakedness. V.25

Praise God for establishing the oneness in the bond of marriage.

iv. **TEACHING METHOD** – Use participatory teaching method.

v. **TIME MANAGEMENT** – Allocate time equally to the two lesson outlines.

2. LESSON OUTLINES

i. **LESSON OUTLINE A** – REQUIREMENTS FOR MARRIAGE PREPARATION

Basic preparations for marriage include:
- Physical and emotional maturity / preparation - Marriage is for matured adult not boys and girls. Ex. 2:1.

Spiritual maturity / preparation- This means:
- Both partners must be born again. I Peter 1:23
- Both must be living a holy life. Heb. 12:14
- Both must be willing to forgive always. Heb. Luke 17:3-4
- Surrendering to divine leading. Psalm 25:9

Financial, material and social maturity/preparation - This is essential at least to meet the basic needs of the family. I Tim. 5:8

CLASS ACTIVITY – Why should the intending couple be matured physically, emotionally, financially and socially?

ii. *LESSON OUTLINE B* – CORRECT CONNECTION

How to have right choice or connection to the right partner include:
- Through the guidance of the Holy Spirit. Psalm 37:23
- Waiting for divine timing, when God will convince you or whisper to you to act. Ecc. 3:1
- Seeking Godly counsels from God's people about right steps to marriage. Proverb 12:15; Pro. 24:6b

3. SUMMARY
Intending couple or youth seeking to enter into marriage relationship must be matured. However, maturity without God is calamity. All planning and execution must be based on God's guidance.

4. CONCLUSION
God must be at the centre of your marriage.

5. ASSIGNMENT
Students should study why God should be fully involved in planning for marriage.

LESSON 44
TO HAVE AND TO HOLD FOR EVER

PRAYER POINT – Father, help every married couple in my Parish to render their duties to their spouses as unto the Lord according to the word of God, in Jesus name.

PREVIOUS KNOWLEDGE – Teacher should allow the students to review the previous week's lesson through guided questions on the Memory Verse, lesson outlines, Summary and Conclusion, etc.

TODAY'S LESSON

1. OPENING

i. ***LESSON TEXT*** – Ephesians 5:22-23

ii. ***MEMORY VERSE*** – "Nevertheless let every one of you in particular so love his wife even as himself; and the wife see that she reverences her husband." Ephesians 5:33

iii. ***LESSON INTRODUCTION*** – Discussions on Christian living will be incomplete without a thorough discussion on marriage and family life. This is an institution that the Lord Jesus Christ likened to the relationship between Him and His Church. May the Holy Spirit teach and bless us the more, in Jesus' name.

TEACHER'S DIARY

i. ***LESSON AIM*** – To study the divine role of the husband, wife and children in family.

ii. ***TEACHING OBJECTIVES AND LESSON PLAN*** – At the end of the lesson, students should be able to understand the divine roles expected from the husband, wife and children in the family. To achieve these objectives students should be able to explain the meaning of submission by women. They should be able to enumerate at least four other qualities expected of a woman by God. They should be able to explain what is meant by husband to love their wives. They should be able to mention some situations under which to express love. They should be able to mention at least five causes of divorce and how to avoid them. To achieve these objectives, students should be encouraged to participate actively in the lesson. Teacher should summarize and conclude the lesson. He should give assignment.

iii. ***TEXT REVIEW*** – Ephesians 5:22-23

    A. "Wives, submit yourselves to your own husbands". Eph. 5:22
- If you submit to Pastor (alone) it is hypocrisy. Matt. 5:23-25
- If you submit to another man it is lust and can lead to adultery.
- If you submit to your friends, it is carnality. I Cor. 3:13
- If you submit to yourself. (lovers of self) It is perilous
- If you fail to submit, it is pride.

    B. "Husband love your wife". Ephesians 5:23
- If you hate your wife, you are a murderer. I John 3:15
- If you do not love your wife, you are unlike Christ.
- If you do not love your wife, you do not love God, you are a liar. I John 4:20.
- If you love another woman, you are adulterous. James 4:4
- If you pretend to love her or to be good to her, you are a hypocrite Matt. 23:27

Failure to obey the two divine orders is a crime against the kingdom and it carries divine penalty. Heb. 13:4

iv. ***TEACHING METHOD*** – Discussion method.

v. ***TIME MANAGEMENT*** – Teacher should use the standard time for teaching three lesson outlines.

2. LESSON OUTLINES

i. *LESSON OUTLINE A* – THE WIFE IN TRUE SUBMISSION

Discuss how the following scriptures can help a Christian wife in true submission.

Teacher Note !

- The words in the brackets are the answers. Do not read them first, let the student read the Bible passages and give their answers, then you can check.
- Teacher can distribute the passages to the students.
- 1 Peter 3:1; Col. 3:18; 1 Tim 2:11-14 (God commanded it)
- Ephesians 5:33 (Reverence the Husband)
- 1 Tim. 2:9-12 (Humility)
- 1 Peter 3:4 (Meekness)
- Titus 2:4-5 (Purity, holiness, love to husband).
- Psalm 128:3, 1 Sam. 2:19 (Mother's heart).
- Proverb 31:30-31 (Diligence and Dependability)
- 2 Kings 4:8-10 (Hospitality)
- Matt. 15:22-28; Acts 1:14 (Prayerfulness)

CLASS ACTIVITY – Examine why some wives find it difficult to submit to their husbands.

ii. *LESSON OUTLINE B* – THE LOVING HUSBANDS

Discuss how the husband should demonstrate that he loves the wife according to the under listed Bible passages:

- Ephesians 5:23, I Cor. 11:3; (As unto Christ)
- Romans 5:6-10 (as Christ loves the Church).
- Ephesians 5:25; (as Christ sacrificed himself for the Church).
- Ephesians 5:28-29 (As the man loves himself)
- Colossians 3:21 (Not to provoke/discourage children).

iii. *LESSON OUTLINE C* – DIVORCE AND GOD'S REMEDY

A. Discuss those things that could lead to divorce.
   - Genesis 2:24, Matt 19:4-6; (Not leaving and cleaving).
   - Eph. 4:27, I Pet. 5:7-9 (Giving place to the devil).
   - I John 4:1 (Giving room to the devil/False prophets).
   - Ephesians 5:22-31; Rom. 12:1-2 (Worldliness/ Extravagance)
   - 2 Cor. 12:5, John 17:20 (Criticisms or lack of forgiveness).
   - Titus 2:4 (Lack of affection)

   B. Teacher should emphasize God's stance on divorce.
   - God forbids divorce. Matt. 19:8
   - Genuine love between couple, tolerance, forgiveness, etc can serve as antidote to divorce. Titus 2:24; Eph. 5:25

3. **SUMMARY**
Marital relationship is forever between couple because God does not give room to divorce. The components of the family have duties for the family.

4. **CONCLUSION**
The family life is a precious relationship ordained by God. How is yours? You can prayerfully answer the question today as you turn to the perfect architect and master builder, that is, the Lord Jesus Christ who can perfect all about your home.

5. **ASSIGNMENT**
Students to study the impact of genuine love between husband and wife on the two and children in the home

LESSON 45
LOVE COVERS ALL

PRAYER POINT – Father, help me to love in words and in deeds, in Jesus name.

PREVIOUS KNOWLEDGE – The Assistant teacher should review the previous week's lesson.

TODAY'S LESSON

1. OPENING

i. ***LESSON TEXT*** – 1 John 4:7-11

ii. ***MEMORY VERSE*** – "And above all these things, put on charity, which is the bond of perfectness." Colossians 3:14

iii. ***LESSON INTRODUCTION*** – Different crimes abound all over the world today and these have led to defilements, shame and sorrows. So also are skirmishes and insurgencies which have led to hunger, displacements and the destruction of many destinies. At the bottom of all these is the absence of love. 2Tim. 3:1-4.

TEACHER'S DIARY

i. ***LESSON AIM*** – To study how love conquers all (adequacies or inadequacies).

ii. ***TEACHING OBJECTIVES AND LESSON PLAN*** – After the lesson, students should be able to mention at least three reasons why love is important. They should be able to enumerate four essentials of love. To achieve these objectives, students should participate actively in the class. Teacher should summarize and conclude the lesson. He should give assignment to the students.

iii. **TEXT REVIEW** – 1 John 4:7-11

Reasons why Christian must love are stated below:
- We are born of God. I John 4:7a
- We know God. I John 4:7a
- God is love. I John 4:8
- God sent Jesus to us because He loved us. I John 4:9a
- We have our lives because He loves us. I John 4:9b
- He sacrificed His son because of love. I John 4:10
- God commanded us to love too. I John 4:11, etc.

Go ahead and love genuinely.

iv. **TEACHING METHOD** – Teacher should use discussion teaching method.

v. **TIME MANAGEMENT** – Teacher should allocate time equally to the two lesson outlines.

2. LESSON OUTLINES

i. **LESSON OUTLINE A** – WHY WE SHOULD TALK ABOUT LOVE
- God is love. I John 4:8
- God loves us and sent Jesus to die for us. John 3:16
- God by His love created us in His own image. Gen. 1:26
- The first and great commandment is love. Matt. 22:37-38
- The second great commandment is love. Matt. 22:37, 39
- All the laws and prophets hang on love. Matt 22:40
- Love is the fulfillment of law. Romans 13:10; John 15:12.

CLASS ACTIVITY – Class should distinguish between genuine love and fake or insincere love.

ii. **LESSON OUTLINE B** – WHAT LOVE ENTAIL

The following are the essentials of love:

- Compassion: This is a strong feeling of empathy for people who are suffering and a desire to help them. Jesus showed compassion throughout His life and ministry here on earth and expects us to do likewise. Matt. 15:32; Luke 7:13.
- Forgiveness: A loving heart is central to forgiveness. Love is not easily offended and it keeps no record of wrongs. A man who loves will always forgive. Eph. 4:32; 1Pet. 4:8.
- Mercy: A kind attitude towards someone that you have the power to harm, punish or ignore. Mercy is possible when love is present. Micah 6:8; Ps. 18:25-26.
- Giving: The act of giving is the best expression of love. The one who loves will present a pleasant offering which is sacrificial and is solving a problem. Jn. 3:16; Rom. 12:13. We can give time, money, encouragement, a listening ear, influence, energy, help, etc.

3. SUMMARY
God is love. He created us in love. He commanded us to love. Love conquers all.

4. CONCLUSION
The word of God says that prophesy and knowledge will fail but love will never fail. We therefore need to cultivate the habit of loving one another for this is God's will for us. 1Cor. 13:1-8.

5. ASSIGNMENT
Students should study how love should be expressed.

LESSON 46
PARENTING IN THE 21ST CENTURY

PRAYER POINT – Father, help all parents not to fail in their responsibility to bring up their children in the way of the Lord, in Jesus name.

PREVIOUS KNOWLEDGE - Teacher should review last week lesson with through guided questions like, "Can someone remind us what the lesson outline one was all about?" "Can another person remind us the memory verse"? etc.

TODAY'S LESSON

1. OPENING

i. ***LESSON TEXT*** – Deuteronomy 6:6-9

ii. ***MEMORY VERSE*** – "For I know him that he will command his children and his household after him, and they shall keep the way of the Lord, to do justice and judgment; that the LORD may bring upon Abraham that which he hath spoken of him." Genesis 18:19

iii. ***LESSON INTRODUCTION*** – Parenting refers to the process of raising and educating a child from infancy to adulthood. Parenting involves parent-child relationship. Parenting can be difficult and challenging, but at the same time the most rewarding and fulfilling things we ever do. The Bible has a great deal to say about the way we can successfully raise our children to be great men and women of God. It is easier to train a child than to repair an adult. Prov. 22:6.

TEACHER'S DIARY

i. ***LESSON AIM*** – To study about parenting in the 21st Century.

ii. ***TEACHING OBJECTIVES AND LESSON PLAN*** – After the lesson, students should be able to mention at least three distinctions between the old and modern ways of parenting. They should be able to enumerate at least three divine expectations on parenting. To achieve these objectives teacher should teach the lesson outlines with appropriate references from the Bible, summarize, conclude and evaluate the lesson. Teacher should give assignment.

iii. ***TEXT REVIEW***: Deuteronomy 6:6-9
- God called the attention of Moses and the children of Israel to the composition of the Great Commandments which are stated in form of commandments, statues and judgements.
- They are to be observed, taught, talked to their generation (parents), the next generation (their sons) and the generations unborn (their son's son) Deut.6:2,7
- The commandment of love of God and love for neighbors must be kept in heart (V.4) in soul (V.4) and might (body) (V.4). They must be taught in the house, on the way, on the bed, and out of the bed. (V.7)
- They must be written on the post of houses, on the gates of compounds, upon hands and upon front heads; V.8-9.
- Remember, the devil too wants to write the signs of the beast upon people's front heads and hands therefore do not give room for devil to write on your hands and head. Revelation 14:9-10

iv. ***TEACHING METHOD*** – Use discussion teaching method.

v. ***TIME MANAGEMENT*** – Teacher should use the standard time for two lesson outlines.

2. LESSON OUTLINES

i. ***LESSON OUTLINE A*** – PARENTING: OLD AND MODERN

    a. Parenting as of old.
- Class should discuss the benefits and weakness of the methods of parenting listed below:

- ◊ The old method of child upbringing which was fashioned after objective criticisms, instilling discipline, home training. Gen.18:19
- ◊ Parenting by example, of good legacy, parenting with the fear of God. Eph. 6:4; Deut.6:2
- ○ Question-Were the old methods of parenting perfect (devoid of error)?
  - ◊ Ans. No. Gideon lacked self-confidence while Hophni and Phinehas were not trained by their father, Eli. I Samuel 3:13 and Judges 6:15

b. Modern Parenting Method

Class should discuss the weaknesses of modern parenting under the following points.

- ○ "What I suffer, my child should not suffer it syndrome".
- ○ Parenting through house help, nannies, electronic gadget, internet, games.etc.
- ○ Parenting by delegation through school teachers, society, religious body.
- ○ Career conscious/non-committed parenting.

CLASS ACTIVITY: Class to identify the weakness or benefits of the above stated parental methods.

ii. *LESSON OUTLINE B* – DIVINE EXPECTATION

God expects that:

- ○ Parents should know and live as God's children in order to lead their children in the way of the Lord. Gen.17:1.
- ○ The parent-child relationship must be based on love and care Eph.6:4.
- ○ Parents should provide for the basic needs (spiritual, material, emotional, educational, etc.) of their children. 1Tim.5:8.
- ○ Parents should relate with their children in truth and openness Prov.12:19.
- ○ Parents should start training their children early. Prov.22:6

- Parents should teach their children the word of God. Deut. 6:6-7
- Parents should apply correction and discipline in love, when and where necessary. However, children should not be abused in the name of correction or discipline Prov. 13:24, 29:15, 17.
- Parents should be good role models. 2Tim.1:5

3. SUMMARY

Both method of parenting (old and modern) have their advantages and limitations, however there are set standards which the Lord expects for parenting which include love, provision of basic need and education, etc. Good parenting will produce good children upbringing.

4. CONCLUSION

God is a parent; a perfect parent, who knows all that parenting entails. It is a great relief to know you are not alone in your parenting responsibility. You can partner with God. Pray and walk with God and He will make you a successful parent indeed.

5. ASSIGNMENT

Identify and discuss forms of child abuse which must be totally discouraged.

LESSON 47
THE MASTER SCULPTOR

PRAYER POINT – Pray that God will make you what He wants you to be.

PREVIOUS KNOWLEDGE – Teacher asks a student to review the previous week's lesson.

TODAY'S LESSON

1. OPENING

i. ***LESSON TEXT*** – Judges 6:11-16

ii. ***MEMORY VERSE*** – "Humble yourselves therefore under the mighty hand of God, he may exalt you in due time" 1 Peter 5:6

iii. A sculptor is an artist who carves or moulds figures, designs and so on in wood, stone, clay, etc. When a sculptor wants to carve out something, he looks at a piece of wood and begins to see what nobody else can see in it. God is the Master Sculptor. In today's lesson, we shall be looking at how God can transform us from logs of wood into beautiful masterpieces.

TEACHER'S DIARY

i. ***LESSON AIM*** – To study how God, the master sculptor, produces a master piece from raw materials.

ii. ***TEACHING OBJECTIVES AND LESSON PLAN*** – At the end of the lesson, students should be able to discover that they are like raw material in the hand of the Master Sculptor and that God engages in a few processes to produce the master piece. To achieve these objectives, the teacher explains how man is like raw materials which need to pass through various processes before he becomes a master piece.

He also explains the process involved in the ultimate transformation of man from raw materials to the finished product.

iii. **_TEXT REVIEW_** – Judges 6:11-16

In the above test, God demonstrated His ability to reform and transform an individual from the present stage to a more desirable stage. For instance:

- Gideon was transformed from being a captive to a captor. Judges 6:14 (thou shall save Israel)
- He was changed from a vanquished to a victor, from a weak and fearful fellow living in a hide out. (Verse 2. verse 6), to a mighty man of valour. verse 2
- God changed him from a poor and mean fellow from Manasseh, to leader and judge of God's people, vs.15, Judges 7:14-25
- He was transferred from the least to the best and from nothing to number one v.15

iv. **_TEACHING METHOD_** – Use participatory and discussion method.

v. **_TIME MANAGEMENT_** – Share teaching time equally between two lesson outlines

2. LESSON OUTLINES

i. **_LESSON OUTLINE A_** – YOU ARE A RAW MATERIAL

The Master Sculptor looks for raw materials to mould and carve.
- He could pick on anybody and make such fellow what He wants him/her to be.
- He picked Gideon as a fearful, coward and victim and made from him a mighty warrior.
- He moulded David from a mere shepherd in the field to become a giant killer.
- He saw a good raw material in Moses at the back side of the desert and made him a great leader.

Peter was a crude fisherman when the Lord picked him to become fisher of men, an apostle for Christ, Luke 5:1-10

Class Activity - Students to share with the class who they were before they met with Christ and who they are after their meeting with Christ.

ii. ***LESSON OUTLINE B*** – THE PROCESSING STAGES

The sculptor engages in some processes to produce a master piece.

NOTE - Teacher identifies the processes and likens them to the process of spiritual transformation.

- The sculptor identifies the correct wood and fetches it. Ex. 3:1-2, 1 Sam. 16:11, Judges 6:11-12. This stage is likened to salvation stage when Jesus locates a sinner.
- The sculptor peels off the back of the tree and where possible, seasons it. This is likened to sanctification of a vessel for the Master use. Acts 9:1-8
- The sculptor commences the carving process with the aid of hammer and chisel. In the spiritual realm, the Holy Spirit uses chisel and hammer to remove covetousness, anger, pride impatience and all unwanted bits which was part of the whole.
- The sculptor uses sandpaper to make his sculptor smooth making rough portions become smooth and pleasing. The word of God does all the sandpapering required to make a fellow pleasing to God.
- The final stage is polishing. This is the manifestation stage when the beauty of the carved is brought to light. The Holy Spirit makes His newly formed individual to begin to manifest the fruit of the Spirit. 2 Sam. 2:4
- A sinner that passes through the above processes would have turned into a saint.

CLASS ACTIVITY 2– Students are asked to mention at least one old behaviour which the Holy Spirit has chiselled out from their lives.

3. SUMMARY

God can mould and re-mould, reform and transform, and bring a saint out of sinner. He can do anything and everything.

4 CONCLUSION

The Lord is looking at you today and speaking into your life and future. He will make up the difference between what you can see and what He can see, which to you is farfetched. Today, yield yourself as that log of wood safely in the arms of the Sculptor.

5 ASSIGNMENT

Form on your table "old" and "new" behaviours from which Christ has transformed you and given glory to God.

LESSON 48
FRUITLESSNESS

PRAYER POINT – Father, help me to be fruitful in all areas of my life in the name of Jesus Christ, Amen.

PREVIOUS KNOWLEDGE – The class teacher should review the previous week's lesson.

TODAY'S LESSON

1. OPENING

  i. ***LESSON TEXT*** – Luke 13:6-9

  ii. ***MEMORY VERSE*** "And now also the axe is laid unto the root of the trees:therefore, every tree which bringeth not forth good fruit is hewn down, and cast into the fire" Matthew 3:10

  iii. ***LESSON INTRODUCTION*** – God is never happy with fruitlessness. Matt. 21:19 because it is against His wish and command. Gen. 1:28. If any branch of the vine is not bearing fruit it will wither or be detached from the vine. Jn. 15:2.

TEACHER'S DIARY

  i. ***LESSON AIM*** – To study the causes and danger of fruitlessness.

  ii. ***TEACHING OBJECTIVES AND LESSON PLAN*** At the end of the lesson, students should be able to enumerate at least four causes of fruitlessness. They should be able to mention at least four dangers of fruitlessness. The class should start with a review of previous week lesson and help students to know the memory verse. Teacher should teach the two lesson outlines with relevant Bible references.

He should summarize, conclude, evaluate and give assignment to the students.

iii. ***TEXT REVIEW*** – Luke 13:6-9
- The expectation of the vineyard owner on the fig tree was dashed when He found no fruit on it, vs. 6
- The owner had for three years waited for the fig to yield fruit but it failed, therefore, it was commanded to be cut down, vs. 7
- But a voice of grace for one more year (this year also) to fertilize it and if is fails, then it shall die, vs. 8-9
- You must realize that the Lord has invested so much on you and I in term of gifts, talents, strength, ability, endowment, money fame, power, blessings, honor, positions, etc for the purpose of satisfying His purpose and need.
- We are mindful of ourselves not minding the one that vested those beautiful grace upon us.
- The voice of grace has been calling quietly for the past three (some) years but now it came with a loud report.
- Imagine what you stand to gain if you are stripped off all the honor and goodness of the Lord for failure to satisfy the one who invested them on you.

iv. ***TEACHING METHOD*** – Teacher should use the lecture teaching method.

v. ***TIME MANAGEMENT*** – Teacher should use the standard time for teaching two lesson outlines.

2. LESSON OUTLINES

i. ***LESSON OUTLINE A*** – CAUSES OF FRUITLESSNESS
- Ignorance and disobedience to God's word. Gen. 1:28; Hos. 4:6a; Matt. 21:28-31a.
- Lack of genuine repentance from sin and other vices, Acts 3:19; Matt. 3:8.

- Pre-occupation with the affairs of this world. Matt. 13:22; 1Jn. 2:16-17.
- Failure to evangelize and win souls. Rom. 1:13, 16; Jn. 15:16.
- Inadequate understanding of the accompanying blessings of fruitfulness. Rom. 10:15; 1Thess. 2:19; Prov. 11:30.

CLASS ACTIVITY – Discuss causes of fruitlessness in God's work among members of your Sunday School Class.

ii. *LESSON OUTLINE B* – DANGERS OF FRUITLESSNESS
- Condemnation, loss and pain Matt. 25:24-30.
- Reversal of blessings. 1Sam. 2:30-34; Mk. 11:12-13
- Separation between God and the fruitless fellow. Rev. 2:4-5
- Self-exposure to attacks. Jonah 1:1-4, 15
- Total destruction of the fruitless fellow. Luke 13:6-9.

3. SUMMARY
There are various causes of fruitlessness and all forms of fruitlessness portend dangers to the victim.

4. CONCLUSION
Just as there are rewards for fruitfulness, there are also consequences for fruitlessness. Rev. 22:11-12. We should be all aspire to be fruitful.

5. ASSIGNMENT
All members of the Sunday School class should work on how to be fruitful in the things of God.

LESSON 49
THE BLEESSEDNESS OF FRUITFULNESS

PRAYER POINT – Father, make me fruitful and multiply, let me replenish the earth and subdue it and have dominion, in Jesus name.

PREVIOUS KNOWLEDGE – Teacher should allow the Assistant Teacher to review the previous week's lesson.

TODAY'S LESSON

1. OPENING

i. ***LESSON TEXT*** – John 15:1-8

ii. ***MEMORY VERSE*** – "And God blessed them, and God said unto them, be fruitful and multiply, and replenish the earth, and subdue it, and have dominion over the fish of the sea, and over the fowl of the air, and over every living thing that moveth upon the earth". Gen. 1:28

iii. ***LESSON INTRODUCTION*** It is the plan of God that man should be fruitful and multiply. Gen. 1:28-29. To be fruitful means being productive in any sense and yielding benefits. Fruitfulness and increase whether in plants and animals depend upon the blessing of God which have allowed the human race to be perpetuated because as one generation passes away another one appears for continuity.

TEACHER'S DIARY

i. ***LESSON AIM*** – To study on the blessings of fruitfulness.

ii. ***TEACHING OBJECTIVES AND LESSON PLAN*** – After the lesson, students should be able to enumerate at least five reasons why fruitfulness is compulsory. They should be able to give at least four expectations on genuine fruitfulness. They should be able to enumerate blessings which follow those who are fruitful. To achieve these objectives, the teacher should introduce the lesson and explain the three lesson outlines. He should summarize, conclude and evaluate the lesson. He should allow active participation of the students. He should not forget to give assignment.

iii. **TEXT REVIEW** – John 15:1-8

- John 15:2 explains the blessing of bearing fruits and the consequences of refusal to bear fruits. Jesus said, "every branch that bear not fruit He takes away while branch which bear fruits He purges it.
- The Lord explained reason for purging the branches in John 15c "that it might bring forth more fruits".
- The Lord spoke further on the means of purging the branch in John 15:3 "Through the word which I spoke to you".

The Lord explained in this passage the secrets behind bearing fruits in the christiandom as follows:

- The fellow must be a branch to the true vine. John 15:1-3
- The branch must remain attached to the true vine. John 15:4
- The vine and the branch must be protected, watered and replenished by the husbandman, God the father. John 15:1
- The branch must be purged and cleaned through the word of God. John 15:3
- The branch must glorify the father to increase from "more fruit" to "much fruit". John 15:2, 8
- Failure to glorify the father by abiding in the son means "nothingness" "withering" and "burning" in fire. John 15:5-6.
- Believers who bear fruit will receive answers to prayers. John 15:7

iv. **TEACHING METHOD** – Teacher should use participatory teaching method.

v. **TIME MANAGEMENT** – Teacher should divide available time equally for the three lesson outlines.

2. LESSON OUTLINES

i. *LESSON OUTLINE A* – WHY WE MUST BE FRUITFUL

Human being must be fruitful for the following reasons:
- It is both a command and a blessing from the Almighty God. Gen.1:28
- It agrees with the divine principle that fruitfulness precedes multiplication. Gen. 17:20; 35:11.
- To be able to disciple or mentor others. 2 Kings 2 :9-12.
- To enjoy a covenant blessing of overflowing fruitfulness on every side. Deut.7:12-14
- To ensure complete compliance of all men to God's will. Matt. 28:18-20

CLASS ACTIVITY – Class should identify those areas where believers are expected to be fruitful.

ii. *LESSON OUTLINE B* – GOD'S EXPECTATION IN FRUITFULNESS

- Be a worthy living epistle to other brethren and believers alike, 2 Cor. 3:1-3
- It serves as an essential proof of the fruit of the Spirit. Gal 5:22-26
- Not forsaking the assembly of one another. Hebrew 10:25
- Covet the usage of the best spiritual gifts. I Cor. 12:8-10
- Be divinely committed to a holy and obedient lifestyle. Acts. 8:26-31, Acts 16:25

iii. *LESSON OUTLINE C* – ACCOMPANYING BLESSINGS OF FRUITFULNESS

The under-listed blessings are some of the benefits and blessings which await those who are fruitful.

- Assurance of answered prayers. John 15:16.
- Unspeakable joy. I Sam. 2:1; Luke 10:17
- A sense of fulfillment. 2 Tim. 4:7-8

- Opportunity to produce more fruits. John 15:3,5
- Divine security is guaranteed to ensure a continuous regular output. John 15:4-6
- Rewards on earth and in eternity. I Tim. 5:18, Matt. 19:27-29.

3. SUMMARY
Fruitfulness is mandatory for believers especially in the spiritual realms. Believers are required to meet God's expectations of genuine fruitfulness. Great blessings await those who are genuinely fruitful.

4. CONCLUSION
Since we have been blessed from the inception by the Almighty God at creation, we should do everything to ensure our fruitfulness so that the blessing would manifest. It is our prayer that God will give us this enabling grace in Jesus name, Amen.

5. ASSIGNMENT
Students should study what is required to turn fruitlessness to fruitfulness.

LESSON 50
OVERFLOWING BLESSINGS

PRAYER POINT – Father, let me experience abundant blessings and life, in Jesus name.

PREVIOUS KNOWLEDGE – Teacher should review the previous week's lesson

TODAY'S LESSON

1. OPENING

  i. ***LESSON TEXT*** – Deuteronomy 28:1-13

  ii. ***MEMORY VERSE*** – "The thief cometh not, but for to steal, and to kill, and to destroy:I am come that they might have life, and that they might have it more abundantly" John 10:10

  iii. ***LESSON INTRODUCTION*** – God wants us to have overflowing blessings. This gives us a picture of blessings without limits Deut. 28:2. Do not place limits on God. Gen 18:14. How much we get from God depends on how much we trust Him Ps. 34:8; Jer. 17:7.

TEACHER'S DIARY

  i. ***LESSON AIM*** – To discover the secret of overflowing blessings.

  ii. ***TEACHING OBJECTIVES AND LESSON PLAN*** – After the lesson, students should be able to mention at least four secrets of overflowing blessings. They should be able to mention at least three ways they can begin to overflow. To achieve these objectives, teacher should review the previous week's lesson and assist the students to carry out the class activities. Teacher should teach the two lesson outlines, summarize, conclude, evaluate the lesson and give assignment. Students should be allowed active participation.

iii. **_TEXT REVIEW_**: Deuteronomy 28:1-13

The Bible passage for today's lesson identified the following manifold blessings for God's children.

- Locational blessing: Blessed in the city. vs. 3
- Occupational blessing: Blessed in the field. vs. 3
- Blessing of Children: Blessed the fruit of thy body. vs. 4
- Agricultural Blessing- Fruit of grounds, increase of animals, vs. 4
- Operational Blessing: Blessed thy baskets and store. vs. 5
- In coming Blessing: Blessed when you come in vs. 6
- Outgoing Blessing: Blessed when you go out. vs. 6
- Victory Blessing: Your enemies shall fall before you. vs. 7
- Vocational Blessing- Blessed on all you lay your hands upon. vs. 7
- Hereditary blessing- Blessed in the land which God gives you. vs. 8
- Covenanted Blessing- Established and be called holy people to Himself. vs. 9
- Identity Blessing- Be called by the name of the Lord. vs. 10
- Abundant Blessing - The Lord will make you plenteous in goods. vs. 11
- Exploration Blessing - God will open to you good treasure. vs.12
- Showers of blessing- God will give you rain. vs. 12
- Prosperity Blessing- Thou shall lend to nations. vs. 12
- Excellence Blessing - The Lord shall make your head only above. vs. 13

Why do not you and your students claim these blessings?

iv. **_TEACHING METHOD_** – Teacher should use the lecture teaching method.

v. **_TIME MANAGEMENT_** – Teacher should use the standard teaching time for two lesson outlines.

2. LESSON OUTLINES

i. *LESSON OUTLINE A* – SECRETS OF OVERFLOWING BLESSINGS

- Be born again. Jn. 3:3; Matt. 6:33.
- Consistent and generous sowing. Prov. 11:24-25.
- Honor the Lord with your tithe and offering. Prov. 3:9-10.
- Diligent obedience. Deut. 28:1.
- Hard work. Prov. 10:4.
- Self-discipline. Job 36:10-11; 1Cor. 9:25.
- Prayers. Jam. 5:16.
- Commitment to God's work. Acts 19:8-12.

CLASS ACTIVITY 1: Class teacher should request the students to rise up and lay their hands on their heads while the teacher pronounces all the blessings listed in the TEXT REVIEW upon them (students) in Jesus name.

ii. *LESSON OUTLINE B* HOW THE OVERFLOW BEGINS

- Accept God's invitation. Jn. 6:35; 7:37-38.
- Get thirsty for God. Matt.5:6; 2 Kgs.2:9-15.
- Be an active soul winner. Jn. 15:16.
- God has already set the table before us and all we need is to key ourselves into it. Ps. 23:5.
- Be a blessing to others. Prov. 22:9.

3. SUMMARY

There are certain secrets which govern overflowing blessings. Some of which are salvation, sowing to God's kingdom, etc. God want believers to commence their overflowing immediately.

4. CONCLUSION

God wants you to have overflowing blessings. The question is what are your expectations? Are you willing to key into the spiritual virtues that will bring this to pass?

5. **ASSIGNMENT**
Students should study and enumerate how believers should use their overflowing blessings.

LESSON 51
HOSPITALITY

PRAYER POINT - Pray that God will help you never to be weary in well doing.

PREVIOUS KNOWLEDGE - Students to explain their understanding on hospitality

TODAY'S LESSON

1. OPENING

i. **LESSON TEXT** – 2 Kings 4:8-18

ii. **MEMORY VERSE** - "Be hospitable to one another without grumbling" 1 Peter 4:9

iii. **LESSON INTRODUCTION** - Hospitality is the friendly and generous reception and entertainment of guest, visitors, or strangers. To be hospitable is to offer a home away from home to meet needs and offer rest to those in need. Paul urged the Corinthian brethren to shelter and support Epaphroditus, one of the brothers in Christ, during his visit to the church in Corinth. Phil 2:28-30. It is our prayer that the Lord will help us to make our home a happy welcome to guest and visitors in Jesus name.

TEACHER'S DIARY

i. **LESSON AIM** – To teach the blessings of being hospitable.

ii. **TEACHING OBJECTIVES AND LESSON PLAN** - At the end of this lesson, students should be able to give four reasons why believers should be hospitable. They should be able to enumerate at least three homes that Jesus Christ visited. They should be able to give five examples of people who gave others hospitality in the scriptures. To achieve these objectives, the teacher should guide the students as they contribute to the lesson. They should add points to the contributions of the students.

iii. **TEXT REVIEW** - 2 Kings 4:8-18
   - There was a notable woman in Shunem, vs. 8
   - Elisha did not go to Shunem because of the woman, vs. 8
   - The woman persuaded Elisha to eat some food, vs. 8
   - Eating by Elisha became a regular occurrence, vs. 8
   - The woman identified Elisha as a holy man of God, vs. 9
   - She persuaded her husband to join in the hospitality of making Elisha comfortable, vs. 10
   - Gahazi had his own role to play, no one is useless, vs. 12
   - Elisha requested to reward the woman for her hospitality by connecting her with notable people in the society, vs. 13
   - The woman did not have any need to mention to Elisha, vs. 13
   - Gahazi noted the only lack in the life of the woman, barrenness with an old husband, vs. 14
   - Elisha prophesized fruitfulness into the life of the woman, vs. 16
   - Though the woman did not believe but she conceived and bore a son according to the words of the man of God, Elisha, vs. 17

iv. **TEACHING METHOD** - Participatory method is recommended for this lesson

v. **TIME MANAGEMENT** - Teacher should allocate equal time to the tree lesson outlines

2. LESSON OUTLINES

i. **LESSON OUTLINE A** - WHY YOU SHOULD BE HOSPITABLE

- You should be hospitable because God commands it, Deut 10:19, Rom 12:13; 15:25-27.
- It is a key to miracles, Gen 18:2-14; 2 Kg 4:8-18.
- You can entertain angels unknowingly when you are hospitable, Heb 13:2.
- Sinner could equally give their lives to Christ when you are hospitable, Lk. 7:36-39; 1 Cor. 10:31; 2 Cor. 9:1
- Add to the list.

ii. ***LESSON OUTLINE B*** - CHRIST WAS ENTERTAINED IN VARIOUS HOMES
- Several people entertained Jesus Christ at different times and different locations.
- Jesus was entertained in the house of Matthew, Mt 9:10.
- He was in the house of Simon the leper, Mk 9:10.
- Jesus was in the house of a Pharisee who requested for His to eat with Him, Lk. 7:36.
- Jesus was entertained by Martha and Mary in the house, Lk 10:38.
- He was also in the house of Zacchaeus, Lk 19:5-7

iii. ***LESSON OUTLINE C*** - INSTANCES OF HOSPITALITY

The following are some instances of hospitality in the Bible
- Abraham's house, Gen 18:4
- Lot's house, Gen 19:2
- Laban's house, Gen 24:31
- Shunammites woman 2 Kg 4:8-18
- Dorcas, Acts 9:36-39
- Lydia, Act 16:15
- Keeper of Prison, Acts 16:34
- Phebe, Rom. 16:1-2
- Churches of Macedonia, 2 Cor. 8:1-4

3. **SUMMARY**

   It is good to be hospitable and don't be weary in well doing for in due course you will reap if you faint not, Gal. 6:9.

4. **CONCLUSION**

   Hospitality is a gift that can open doors to our needs and miracles. God wants us to be a generous and a true giver. He is always doing something in return to our gracious hospitality. When we encounter brethren and men of God who can benefit from our support, we should not hesitate to offer hospitality.

5. **ASSIGNMENT**

   Each class to plan being hospitable to the nearest homeless nearest to the church.

LESSON 52

THE FOURTH QUARTER INTERACTIVE SESSION

Welcome to the Fourth Interactive Session!

Your privileges:

- ○ To ask questions on treated lessons for clarity
- ○ To give critical appraisal of the outline
- ○ To give useful suggestions towards better performance
- ○ To give useful spiritual contributions

Errol & Deborah
Manwarren

CPSIA information can be obtained
at www.ICGtesting.com
Printed in the USA
LVOW01s0914210816
500703LV00002B/2/P

9 781609 241247